Why Choose the Episcopal Church?

revised edition

———

John M. Krumm

Forward Movement Publications
Cincinnati, Ohio

revised edition

ISBN 0-88028-169-3
Order no.: 531

Original edition, copyright 1957, by John McGill Krumm. Published by Thomas Nelson and Sons, New York, 1957, under the title "Why I Am An Episcopalian." Revised for the Forward Movement Publications' editions of 1974 and 1996.

About the Author

John McGill Krumm was chairman of the Executive Committee of Forward Movement Publications from 1976 to 1991, then vice-chairman until five weeks before his death in 1995. He had, from 1971 to 1980, been Bishop of Southern Ohio and had served as a member of the Joint Commission on Ecumenical Relations and chairman of the Episcopal Church delegation to COCU. From 1980 to 1985 he was Bishop-in-charge of the Convocation of American Churches in Europe. Earlier in his ministry he served as Rector of St. Matthew's, San Mateo, and Dean of St. Paul's Cathedral, Los Angeles; then Chaplain of Columbia University and Rector of the Church of the Ascension in New York City. He earned a Ph.D. in history from Yale University and was well known as a lecturer, preacher and author of numerous books, pamphlets and articles, including *Flowing Like a River, Modern Heresies, The Art of Being a Sinner* and (with Marion Kelleran) *Denver Crossroads*.

———

For Karin Perkins

with the author's gratitude for an efficient and delightful chauffeur in Nuremberg 20-21 August 1983.

—John M. Krumm

Contents

Introduction

At the university where I was Chaplain every entering student was invited to state what the registration form referred to as a "religious preference." It is interesting to speculate as to what that phrase "religious preference" really means. How have most of us arrived at the particular spiritual household where we now abide? The term "religious preference" may be misleading if it suggests that we have carefully examined all the possible religious alternatives and then made a judicious selection based on our own taste and temperament or on the inherent persuasiveness of the religious position itself. Such a meaning for "religious preference" is misleading because this is not at all the way in which most of us have found our way into our religious affiliation.

As a matter of fact, many students at any university state as their religious preference the affiliation of their parents, and they do not mean to imply that they have given this affiliation any very careful scrutiny. Even those who have formed an ecclesiastical or religious connection with some show of independence will admit that all kinds of circumstantial factors have played a major part in their action. A chance acquaintance with some minister, the invitation of a friend or neighbor, the convenient location or attractive appearance of some church building—these are the factors which many of us would confess had most to do with our "religious preference." To an outsider all this will appear to be mere happenstance. If I had not moved to a certain town, known a certain friend, met a certain minister, I would not be an Episcopalian at all, the supposedly weighty arguments of this book notwithstanding.

Because, however, these apparently arbitrary personal experiences have led to the apprehension of deeply significant truth, the believer can never put them down to mere luck or chance. We shall always say with St. Paul, "By the grace of God, I am what I am." While I must confess that I became a Christian within the fold of the Episcopal Church and the Anglican Communion through a series of personal experiences of a seemingly arbitrary sort, I must also insist that I remain an Episcopalian gladly and enthusiastically because in and through these personal experiences the Spirit himself has led me to profound and persuasive truth.

In this book is the description of what the Episcopal Church has come to mean to me, how it appears to me to combine in one inclusive formulation of faith and experience so many aspects of the truth about

God and man and their relationship one with another. It would, of course, be quite out of keeping with the spirit of the Christian fellowship to make disparaging or invidious comparison between my own church and other communions. At the same time, I must plainly warn the reader that I do not consider religious connection and association to be merely a matter of taste, much as some people prefer black olives and other people green. Ultimately I am an Episcopalian not because it suits me, for it does not always do so exactly and indeed sometimes irritates me very much indeed. I am an Episcopalian ultimately because I believe that in this church and Communion the great truth of Christianity is most adequately and fully set forth in balance and proportion and that through its life of worship and witness it makes possible the richest kind of fellowship with God and with my fellowmen. That I was drawn to this church I regard as the leading of a gracious and provident God, and I am glad to be able to try to tell what he taught me and showed me in this experience.

—J.M.K.

One

How It Happened

It is probably significant that I came in touch with the Episcopal Church because of an invitation to take a leading part in its worship. The invitation had about it something of the nature of a bribe. A friend down the street whose mother helped to play the piano for choir practice at the local Episcopal Church urged me to join him in a new boys' choir that was to be organized and rehearsed in time to sing for the Christmas Eve service. He pointed out that recruits to this choir were to be rewarded after Christmas by a free trip from our southern California town to San Francisco, which I had never seen. It sounded like a good idea.

I had very few religious prejudices that interfered with considering this proposition. My father's family were strongly committed Missouri Synod Lutherans, in which church I had been baptized. The Sunday school curriculum of that church was not very attractive to a small boy. It consisted of memorizing large portions of Luther's Short Catechism. Today I have a healthy and mature respect for Luther's theology, but its excitement and relevancy did not quite reach me in those rather boring years of Sunday school. The only time I remember being interested was when we were allowed—only once as I recall—to go into church for a part of the worship. My memory recalls the mysterious height of the Gothic roof and the distant lights of the altar area. But that visit to the church did not recur, and in the meantime, the children next door offered to take me to their Sunday school, where they assured me things were much more interesting. Perhaps because this relieved my parents of driving all the way across town to deposit me at the Lutheran Sunday school, I was allowed to switch my allegiance to what turned out to be the Methodists. My chief memory of that period in my Christian education was starring in the role of the boy with the loaves and fishes in a Sunday school pageant, put on for the congregation at the time of their major Sunday service. Soon afterwards we moved to Southern California, and once again the Methodist Sunday school wooed me successfully by featuring me in a chalk-talk sermon on "The Love of Money as the Root of All Evil." There had already been intimations that it was about time I considered joining the Methodist Church, when my chum down the street outlined the advantages— looming largest was the trip to San Francisco—of becoming involved in the Episcopal Church.

I was immediately glamorized by the Episcopal Church. I rather liked to sing. Getting "dressed up" in vestments appealed to my vanity. Our debut performance on Christmas Eve was a whole new revelation of what going to church might mean. It was a dramatic and awesome experience, and even though the trip to San Francisco never materialized I was hopelessly and irrevocably intrigued by my new church connection. After a few months I heard that the bishop was coming to confirm and to dedicate the impressive new church building, and one afternoon when I came home from school I found the rector talking to my mother about whether I might attend confirmation classes. I was flattered that he wanted me to be confirmed and agreed at once when my mother said the decision was up to me. The bishop's visit was all I had hoped and expected it to be. He was an unusually impressive and dignified man with a gloriously deep voice. As he laid his hands on my head I felt that something very, very important was happening. The rector in the confirmation class had reminded us that the bishop himself had hands laid on his head in his ordination and consecration as a bishop, and that this chain of laying on of hands stretched way back to the earliest days of the church. I had a dim sense that I was part of something very ancient as I knelt at the altar rail that Sunday morning.

Within a year and a half of my confirmation my family moved about ten miles away to another community in Southern California, but I headed straight for a nearby Episcopal Church, no longer able to sing treble in the choir but eager to get involved in other ways in what I had found to be an extraordinarily congenial church home. I taught Sunday school, joined the high school youth fellowship, became a lay reader, and returned to choir singing, this time as a baritone. Soon the rector began to suggest that I might consider the ordained ministry as my life work. There was no denying that it had great appeal to me, but I was reluctant to decide at once, and the rector made no effort to push me.

In the meantime the economic depression of the early 1930's grew worse and worse. My own family suffered considerably, and I felt indignation and outrage that hard-working people should be victimized and humiliated. The social witness of Christianity appealed to me greatly, and one year I taught a Sunday school class about the Hebrew prophets, drawing a parallel between the farm workers then on strike in the Imperial Valley and Amos's description of the harassment and exploitation of the poor in 8th century B.C. Israel. Some parents protested to the rector, but he upheld the policy of "academic freedom" even for a college freshman Sunday school teacher. Some of the pronouncements of the House of Bishops at that time, especially a ringing denunciation in a Pastoral Letter issued in 1933 of the callousness and inequities of our economic life, stirred me deeply. The then bishop of the Episcopal Church in San Francisco,

Edward L. Parsons, became one of my heroes, as did the suffragan bishop of Los Angeles, Robert B. Gooden.

As was the case with many college students, my days at the university tested my Christian beliefs and commitments severely. The modesty and confidence of the committed Christians on and around the campus, however, impressed me and tipped the balance in favor of the Christian church. I worked in my senior year in the religious center, cleaning offices, serving meals, typing and manning the office switchboard. I became acquainted with a wide spectrum of church leaders from the YMCA to the Roman Catholics. They struck me as an unusually honest and frank group of people, admitting that some aspects of the faith bothered and confused them, but bearing witness to the importance in their own lives of the things they did believe strongly and unmistakably. My decision to go into the ministry was becoming more and more inevitable, and I called on the bishop who encouraged me to persevere. I shifted my major to philosophy and enjoyed enormously getting acquainted with Augustine, Anselm, and Aquinas as well as the religious philosophies of Royce and Bergson and James and other moderns. In my senior year I had made my decision about going to seminary, and was accepted at the Virginia Theological Seminary in Alexandria.

It was a demanding curriculum and a faculty with some very exciting teachers. More than that, it was a seminary strong in the evangelical tradition, laying great emphasis on personal religious experience. I did not abandon my "social gospel" concerns of the college years, but I found them deepened and strengthened by a solid basis of devotion and theology. The world around us in the late 1930's was growing ominously dark with the shadow of Hitler's Germany casting itself over the optimism of my earlier years. Albert T. Mollegen was just beginning his teaching career at Virginia which was to last for 38 years. He drew together world history and the insights and faith of the Bible in a remarkable and unforgettable way, interpreting it all with a vigorous life of devotion and prayer and salting it with his own delightful humor and his incredible patience with students. The biblical scholarship of Stanley Brown-Serman, the familiarity with Church history of Alexander Zabriskie, the thorough scholarship in the history of Christian thought of Charles Lowry—all this and more gave me a balanced and rich introduction to the intellectual side of Christianity.

In the years that have followed (58 by now) no one could have had a more varied ministry—in three little blue collar towns of Southern California, a curacy in a New Haven parish during two years of graduate study at Yale Divinity School, an historic congregation in an affluent San Francisco suburb, the cathedral in downtown Los Angeles with a special responsibility for the elderly people who lived all around us, the chaplaincy of Columbia University, a medium sized Fifth Avenue congregation, and then bishop of a lively and vigorous diocese—it has given me the opportunity to test the rather superficial attractions I had first experienced for the Episcopal Church against the needs of all sorts of people. It has satisfied me and others to whom I have ministered in all kinds of ways—devotionally, liturgically, theologically, intellectually, prophetically, pastorally. The only importance of telling what the Episcopal Church came to mean to me is that it may illustrate the different kinds of needs and experiences which this major Christian tradition can meet and satisfy. The rest of this book will seek to show how this is so.

Two

Worship

For me, as for many others in the Episcopal Church, the most important single impression it made was of the dignity and objectivity of its worship. My experiences with American protestant worship had not, of course, been very wide. I had known a variety of Sunday schools and had found them rather boring as far as experiences of genuine worship were concerned. For the most part, the stress was on a study of the Bible, and what might be called worship was encompassed in a rather monotonous series of brief and shapeless "opening exercises." Surely our protestant programs of Christian education have often been seriously lacking at this point. When one realizes that for the greater part of its history the Christian church has relied upon the experience of common worship to convey the meaning and significance of its faith, one becomes keenly aware of how impoverished any program of Christian training and nurture must inevitably be which lacks opportunities for introduction to and training in Christian worship. If a certain Lutheran Sunday school had paid somewhat less attention to Luther's Short Catechism and a little more to the authentic Lutheran liturgical genius, I might never have been an Episcopalian at all!

For the most part, however, even the adult congregation in most American protestant churches participates in a life of worship which only very partially meets some of the criteria of an authentic Christian worship. In the first place, my experience with the worship of most protestant churches has convinced me that the element most often lacking might be identified as "objectivity." For the most part the congregation is the object of primary attention and their edification is thought of as the chief purpose of the church service. The traditional church architecture which is universally employed in Episcopal churches suggests at once to the person who comes into the church building that such is not the case here. At the center of the church building is the altar and the cross and the attention and respect paid to this area of the church building is symbolic of a genuine sense of the presence and reality of God in the midst of his people. As a choir boy I was instructed carefully about bowing reverently to the altar when I passed in front of it, keeping outside the altar rails unless some business directly connected with worship took me inside, facing toward the liturgical eastern end of the church where the altar was located to recite the Apostles'

Creed, and in other ceremonial acts. No one made a great point about it but I was impressed forcibly with the fact that here was a kind of Christianity that realized that God was the mysterious center of Christian worship and the fact that a congregation was present was only important insofar as it served to praise and glorify him.

Many years later I read a charming story by Cecil B. de Mille in which he told of an occasion during his childhood when he went to a Lenten service in the nearby Episcopal church, only to discover to his terror and surprise that he was the only member of the congregation! Before he had time to flee, however, the rector had entered the chancel and was beginning Evening Prayer. Mr. de Mille recorded the deep impression that this clergyman's conduct of the service made upon the little boy who constituted his entire congregation. The whole service was read through carefully and reverently, just as if the church were filled with worshipers. Mr. de Mille realized that there was an attitude toward worship that regarded God as the center of it all and whether there were two worshipers or two thousand was a matter of relative indifference.

Equally impressive to me was the assumption that worship was an activity in which the congregation took an active part. Gradually there dawned upon me the significance of the fact that in the Episcopal Church the place where the congregation sits is not called an "auditorium." The congregation is not there just to "audit;" they are there to worship. There are important things for them to do. They have parts of the service to say. They attest to their meaningful participation in the service by standing, kneeling, and sitting down at the appropriate places. It was a great relief to a small boy—as it has continued to be a relief to a mature man—to know that worship was something that one could participate in by saying certain things and doing certain things quite independent of special religious or spiritual feelings or sentiments. God is glorified by any conscientious and honest act of adoration even if the heart is lukewarm and the mind dulled with weariness. Since worship is something offered to God and not something primarily designed to induce religious experiences in the worshiper, an Episcopalian is mercifully relieved of the appalling responsibility of trying to feel pious and spiritual. It was not that strong sentiments did not occasionally overcome me, and still do in surprising and unexpected moments in worship—but that such experiences were quite incidental to the main business of worship.

I found that what is true of any art is true also of worship—it creates its deepest effect when it is least concerned with effect, it has its greatest power when it is most completely dedicated to the purity and integrity of its art. To hear a group of boy choristers singing the Psalms in Westminster Abbey can transport me into the seventh heaven, but it does so precisely because the choristers are completely caught up in the task of rendering as purely and beautifully as they can the words and music of the text to the praise and glory of God. The rediscovery of the art of worship in protestantism has been marred to some extent by a kind of self-conscious theatricalism which often seems to have as its primary object creating what is rather barbarously called "a worship experience." It must be confessed that in some Episcopal churches this same corrupting and degrading idea is also to be found. The real art of worship will never come into its own until it loses its self-consciousness and seeks as its chief object the pure and unalloyed adoration and worship of Almighty God.

In order to secure the ends and results described above, the Episcopal Church has always been dedicated to the principle of liturgical worship. While the exact derivation of the word is somewhat uncertain, there is evidence to suggest that the word "liturgy" derives from two Greek words *laos*, meaning "people," and *ergos*, meaning "work." The liturgy is that which the people do together. Since this is the case there must be prescribed rules and agreed upon forms by which the service proceeds. Only in a service which the worshiper can depend upon to move in a certain way and to take a certain form will the worshiper be sufficiently at home to take a lively and intelligent part. So-called "extemporaneous" prayer or "free worship" inevitably produces a kind of hesitancy on the part of the congregation because of the uncertainty as to what is going to happen next.

It must be confessed that the result of the use of such forms of worship, agreed upon and universally employed, is sometimes a kind of empty formalism. This is perhaps all the more dangerous because of the magnificent but oftentimes obscure 16th and 17th-century English in which most of the prayer book is written.

The 1979 prayer book guards against this danger in two ways—by translating the 16th and 17th century language into modern equivalent language, and secondly, by providing a variety of eucharistic prayers. Both these safe-guards, however, have their own drawbacks. Translation is a rare gift, not bestowed on all revisers of the prayer book; one example of an admirable translation is the 1979 Psalter. Credit to whom credit is due: the Rev. Dr. Charles Guilbert, for many years secretary of the House of Deputies of the General Convention. Not only does he make the original meaning clear but the dignity and rhythm of the traditional English psalter is admirably preserved. Not everything in the 1979 book is so successful. An otherwise excellent litany of "Thanksgiving for National Life" is spoiled by the abrupt responses (cf. page 838) "Hear us," "Forgive us," "Inspire us" etc. By adding words like "Good Lord" or "O Lord" the flow and the rhythm would add immeasurably to the dignity of the language.

The second principle that saves the congregation from hearing familiar words but missing their impact is the use of a variety of different eucharistic prayers. Including both Rite I and Rite II, there are six possibilities for a eucharistic rite, and the casual visitor, unless a printed guide for the service is provided, is hopelessly lost. This may minimize "wanderings of mind," but it may leave the congregation scrambling to find the right page with little opportunity to reflect upon the deeper meaning of the worship.

The 1979 prayer book presupposes a fairly well disciplined and instructed group of worshipers. Does this correspond, however, to the reality of the average Sunday morning congregation? Often it does not, especially in a metropolitan setting. "Casual visitors" may be reading these pages. Many of them have had experience with non-liturgical worship in congregations of protestant traditions. The frequency of celebrations of the Eucharist, for example, is not what they are used to. They are more comfortable in a service of reading and exposition of scripture and brief prayers, interspersed with the singing of chants and familiar hymns. The present prayer book says, quite properly, that the Holy Eucharist is "the principal act of worship on the Lord's Day" (page 13). It does not say, however, that it must be the *only* act of Christian worship on the Lord's Day. Why do not more clergy and worship committees take seriously the rubric on page 36: "At celebrations of the Holy Eucharist, the order for Morning and Evening Prayer may be used in place of all that precedes the offertory." This is done in some congregations and in most of the cathedrals in England and has much to recommend it. The 1979 prayer book is a wonderfully rich treasury of forms of liturgical worship. Why do so many congregations fall into a routine which makes use of only part of the possibilities? Why, for example, is Morning Prayer or Rite I almost never heard on Sunday mornings in some congregations? If you choose the Episcopal Church, speak up and claim the full heritage that is provided in the prayer book.

One of the chief advantages of liturgical worship lies in the insurance it gives of balance and proportion. Free worship and extemporaneous prayer rarely (except in the case of the few individual clergymen who are geniuses in the art of public worship) achieve the level of excellence in these respects that is everywhere evident in the services of the Book of Common Prayer. Each service has its own "rationale"—an orderly plan by which the service proceeds through a number of phases and expresses the whole range of Christian worship.

Not only does each prayer book service proceed according to a carefully balanced plan of its own, but through the use of the traditional Christian calendar the services during the year stress first one and then another of the main biblical themes in such a way as to bring the whole Christian story to the attention of the worshiper. In Advent the significance of Christ for the ultimate issues of human life and history is stressed; in the Christmas and the Epiphany seasons the reality and meaning of Jesus Christ's coming into human life; in Lent the sharp challenge which Christ's life presents to the easy-going ways of the world, a challenge which becomes dramatically focused in the events of Passiontide and Holy Week; on Good Friday and Easter the triumphant reassurance of God's ultimate victory even in the crises of suffering, failure, and death; in Ascensiontide the ultimate authority of Christ and his kingdom over the whole creation; in Whitsuntide the ongoing work of Christ through the person of the Holy Spirit, especially within the life and fellowship of the Christian church; and in the long sequence of Sundays after Pentecost the meaning of this great Christian story for our whole attitude toward life and its problems and opportunities. So the Christian year is simply the way in which the Episcopal Church expresses its concern that the whole of the Bible in its main emphases shall engage the attention of the Christian worshiper throughout a twelve-month period. Rather than depending upon the range of interests of any given clergyman, influenced by the many pressures which crowd the calendar with days of civic or community concern, the Episcopal Church by its careful adherence to the traditional Christian calendar ensures for its worshipers the perennial exercise of hearing again the great Christian story in its fullness.

Formalism is the occupational disease of any Christian worshiper, no matter whether he be committed to the principle of extempore prayer or to liturgical prayer. Who has not known clergymen of the "free church" tradition who in their so-called "extemporaneous" prayers repeated hackneyed and meaningless phrases with a formalism that equaled or exceeded that of the most unimaginative advocate of liturgical worship. Part of my early ministry was spent in a community which was in those days a singularly drab and cheerless place, the dumping ground of unfortunate victims of the depression of the 1930's, a place of sub-standard housing, organized gambling, and general dreariness. One of the local ministers, whenever called upon to lead in prayer at community or civic ceremonies, invariably began with the words "O God, we thank thee for 'Blankville.'" It occurred to me many times that God had had all too little to do with the development of "Blankville" and that in any case he didn't deserve much credit for it! Surely here was formalism, and what is more a formalism based upon a fairly barren and unimaginative literary pattern.

To lead liturgical worship does require constant vigilance. The very existence of a pattern and form of words can be temptation to careless preparation and sloth. However, a conscientious clergyman or individual worshiper, by a certain amount of thoughtful preparation and careful attention over a period of years to the familiar words which stand before him in the pages of the prayer book, will find himself entering into one of the richest treasure houses of Christian devotion and piety to be found anywhere in the English language outside the pages of the Bible itself.

If I were to cite one single reason why I became and still remain an Episcopalian, I think I would point to the Book of Common Prayer and to its universal acceptance in the Anglican communion as the basis for Christian life and worship.

One of the dangers in organized religion in America is that it will buy popularity by appealing only to the immediately felt needs of people. Biblical religion, on the contrary, has often told people that their felt needs are far from measuring the real depths of their problems. The prayer book has seemed to me more and more to be the best guarantee that the real dimensions of the human problem and the real clue to its resolution will continue to be set before the congregation of God's people Sunday after Sunday, week in and week out, in a balanced and orderly way. Whatever the minister may say or fail to say in his sermon, no congregation using the Book of Common Prayer will for long accept any easy solution of the problems of human existence nor any watered down estimate of the true goal of human life. The profundities of the confession, the burial office, the moving language by which the sacraments of Holy Baptism and the Holy Communion are celebrated and administered—all of this and much else besides in this great depository of Christian devotion and aspiration rebukes the easy amiability of a moralistic pulpit and the "get-spiritual-quick" ambition which often infects the pew. A liturgical life which initially attracted me by its dignity and beauty now appeals to me most deeply as a way of mediating to a congregation the genuine depth and richness of the biblical view of life.

Theoretically this might be provided by a painstaking and thorough-going reading of the Bible undertaken by an individual on his own, but as a matter of practice for most church members this is hardly a live option. To worship by the prayer book—which in itself draws heavily upon biblical material or upon paraphrasings of it—is to confront the biblical faith, epitomized and made concrete in terms of perennial Christian needs and concerns. The widespread use, for example, of the Book of Common Prayer even among churches of the "free worship" tradition on occasions such as burial and marriages, indicates the success it has had in rendering the biblical faith in a convenient and usable way as the theme and motif of Christian worship and life. To be able to take for granted in the regular worshiping life of the church the magnificence of a prayer book has always seemed to me one of the great glories of the Episcopal Church.

Three

Sacraments

I have tried to say in the last chapter that one of the attractions of the Episcopal Church for me was the element of objectivity in its worship. This objectivity is seen most clearly in the sacramental character of the life of an Episcopalian. In its broadest meaning, our whole world is sacramental. That is to say, every time I shake you by the hand, or salute the flag, or put on an academic cap and gown and hood, I am illustrating the prevalence of the principle that outward and visible actions and things serve to convey spiritual meanings. We shall see in the next chapter that the Episcopal Church makes maximum use of this principle, which is written into nature and the longest standing customs of human society. Color, architecture, gesture, music, vestments—all these things can be used for the greater glory of God.

The prayer book defines a sacrament, however, in a more precise way: ". . . outward and visible signs of inward and spiritual grace, given by Christ as sure and certain means by which we receive that grace." Two sacraments have a clear claim to primary attention on this definition, being plainly "ordained by Christ himself" in the pages of the New Testament; these are Holy Baptism and the Holy Communion.

The Episcopal Church, following the usage of an over-whelming majority of present-day Christian churches and of the almost unanimous verdict of the church down through the ages, practices infant baptism. Here again the objectivity of Anglican worship is demonstrated. God can work an all-important change in a person's life long before the person is aware of it. This seems such a plain fact in other areas of life that one wonders why it was ever questioned in the area of religion. A child is a member of his family from the day he opens his eyes. He will know nothing of the family's name or its standards or its ideals or its history for many years to come. This does not mean that from the very beginning he is not participating in a very real sense in that family's life and is not receiving from his membership in it all kinds of formative and determinative influences. He may later prove unworthy of the family. He may flout its finest traditions and renounce any responsibility for its life, but he can never deny that he belongs to that family and belonged to it from the day he was born. The Episcopal Church and other churches which practice infant baptism take a similar view of Holy Baptism. It makes a child a member of Christ; it draws him into the environment of Christ's household and family, the church; it initiates a process that, quite without the child's knowing it, will shape and form his life and his attitudes. Can anyone deny that this child is a member of the church? The Episcopal Church at least dares not deny it, and believes it is following the Spirit of its Lord who rebuked the disciples when they sought to hinder children from coming to him and assured them of a welcome place in his presence and company.

The Episcopal Church follows carefully the New Testament directions for the administration of Holy Baptism, using invariably water and the formula of the invocation of the Holy Trinity ("In the name of the Father and of the Son and of the Holy Spirit"). Indeed, any baptism which is administered in this way is accepted as a valid baptism, no matter where or by whom performed. Following the ancient usage of the early church, established when life was somewhat uncertain and the possibility of a baptized child coming inadvertently into the care of a pagan family was very real, the Episcopal Church makes use of the institution of godparents. Since the duties of the godparents are very important as a part of the presuppositions of the administration of the sacrament of Baptism, most Episcopal clergy require that the godparents themselves be baptized persons, or at least receive some instruction in their duties and responsibilities and express a ready willingness to discharge them faithfully.

The prayer book makes no mention of the

possibility—except in a grave emergency—of a Baptism being held anywhere but in the church building itself. The growing custom of holding Baptisms at a time when the majority of the congregation can be present has everything to commend it—excepting only the consequent anxiety of proud mothers lest the little candidate disgrace the family "before all those people!" Baptism is not some magical rite of mysterious significance; it has the plain and obvious—albeit incalculable—effect of initiating the child into the new environment of the Christian family of the church. What is more natural than that the members of this wider family shall be present on such an auspicious occasion? Anxious mothers ought to realize that congregations will usually tolerate even fairly obstreperous infants and still be moved by the spectacle of initiating a new Christian into the church of twenty centuries. The Episcopal Church follows the ancient church's custom of beginning the observance of the great Easter festival by the administration of Holy Baptism, usually late on the afternoon of Easter Even or, more often in recent years, in the full observance of the Easter Vigil.

Baptism is the sacrament of Christian initiation; the Holy Communion is the sacrament of Christian sustenance and renewal. From the earliest times it has been regarded as the central act of worship in the Christian community. The Apology of Justin Martyr, for example, written in the middle of the second century, describes it as the characteristic way in which Christians express their faith and their devotion. Incidentally, Justin's description sounds remarkably like any celebration of the Holy Communion in an Episcopal parish, even to the use of the ancient formula, "Lift up your hearts," and the response, "We lift them to the Lord," as a prelude to the act of consecrating the bread and wine. The Holy Communion holds this central place in Christian life and worship because it so superbly sums up and expresses the deepest Christian convictions about God and human life.

The Liturgy begins with a salutation and response and moves on to a prayer which is a reminder of how much true worship depends upon inward qualities of mind and heart which God alone can inspire and recognize and judge. ("God . . . unto whom all hearts are open, all desires known, and from whom no secrets are hid.") This is usually followed by the ancient hymn "Gloria in excelsis" or the briefer "Kyrie Eleison" or some other suitable hymn ("gloria" is usually omitted on penitential occasions, including the season of Lent). Then come the "propers"—the prayer and the Bible readings assigned by the church calendar. The sermon follows directly upon the reading of the Gospel and is obviously intended normally to be an exposition of a theme found in one or more of the biblical selections.

At major services the sermon reaches a climax in the Nicene Creed, the ancient formula by which the church confessed her common faith and trust in God (hence "We believe") based upon his disclosure of himself in creation, in the coming into history of Jesus Christ his eternal Son, and in the continuing guidance, inspiration, and empowerment of the Spirit. This reminder in scripture, sermon, and creed of all that God has done and continues to offer to do for us brings the Christian worshiper to a sense of his own, his community's, and the church's denials, refusals, and betrayals of the divine love and purpose. Normally there follows, therefore, a confession of sin and a formal absolution which invokes God's promised forgiveness and acceptance of us despite all our neglect, failure, and mistakes. Then, because we ought never come to the Holy Communion without carrying along with us a concern for the needs and perplexities of others, we share our intercessions for the world and the church and for all men and women everywhere. Before we proceed to the Offertory, Consecration, and Communion the ceremony of the exchange of the Peace is performed (though the place of this ancient expression of Christian fellowship and mutuality in the Liturgy may vary from one congregation or act of worship to another).

Then the offering follows—not just an embarrassing necessity if the utilities are to be paid and the minister's salary kept up—but an expression of the fact that God welcomes man's gifts of himself, of his labor, of his capacity and strength. In Justin's day there was very little money in circulation—especially among poorer people like the Christians—and so the offering was often bread and wine, gifts in kind, as we should say. Today in many Episcopal Churches this ancient symbolism is maintained as men and women bring up from the congregation at the offering time not only the gifts of money but also the very bread and wine which are to be used in the Holy Communion. The bread and the wine are symbols of the gifts of God's creation, moulded and shaped and made usable by the talent and skill and intelligence of men and women.

We are ready now to bless and consecrate these gifts and make them the means by which God's love and power can enter more fully into our lives. Like ancient Judaism, the church blesses by giving thanks, by ascribing to God the glory and the virtue of life. "Let us give thanks," says the priest, again using the language of St. Justin's description, and the people respond: "It is right to give him thanks and praise." Then in the solemn prayer of consecration and in the poignant act of breaking the bread the priest recalls to us the offering that God made in Christ, an offering that covers the inadequacies of our offerings, so that God can take our offerings and give them back to us in the act of communion, with the assurance that we are receiving now the very substance of our Lord's life into our lives. "The Body of our Lord Jesus Christ, which was given for thee, preserve thy body and soul unto everlasting life" or "The Body of Christ, the Bread of Heaven." After a brief prayer of thanksgiving and the blessing, the service is over, and the people are sent out into the world to live more fully as Christ's own men and women.

What could more eloquently portray the deepest realities of the Christian life—God's demands, God's offer, our offerings, our sin, God's forgiveness, new power to live in him, with him in us? The Episcopal Church is content that men shall find these realities in her service of the Holy Communion, and does not press precise definitions as to just what happens or how it happens. There is no definition of the doctrine of Christ's presence in the Holy Communion, although in the Articles of Religion the definition of Transubstantiation is rejected as inconsistent with the church's understanding of a sacrament. (Apparently the compilers of the Articles believed that the doctrine of Transubstantiation implied the view that when God makes use of material things he must destroy their inner reality. Such a view they declared is in effect to "overthrow the nature of a sacrament" and to deny the essential compatibility between nature and spirit which the whole sacramental principle is intended to express and defend.) It is abundantly clear that the prayer book believes that Christ is present in the Holy Communion—although it will not define just how or just when or just where. Episcopalians differ on these matters and have differed for hundreds of years.

What is more important is that the Holy Communion continues to be the center of the church's worshiping life; it is the natural expression in high festival moments like Christmas and Easter or in other moments of corporate or personal significance—at the consecration of a bishop or the ordination of a deacon or a priest, at a marriage or a funeral, in times of sickness and distress—of the Christian faith in Christ and his power to heal and forgive and save. No words can describe what an Episcopalian finds Sunday after Sunday, day after day, year in and year out, as he brings to the altar rail his problems, his joys, his successes, his failures, his sins, his victories over temptation and despair. Our status as God's children; our status as brothers and sisters of another; our status as heirs of the promises of a fulfillment which will exceed all that we can desire—all this is reaffirmed every time we come to be fed with Christ's own life. This is the heart and center of the Christian life, and every Episcopalian is grateful for the long tradition he has inherited which magnifies its importance and multiplies the opportunities for its celebration.

"What are the two great sacraments of the Gospel?" asks the Catechism. The answer is: "The two great sacraments given by Christ for our salvation are Holy Baptism and the Holy Eucharist." Some Episcopalians, following the rather arbitrary numbering of Peter Lombard in the Middle Ages, say there are seven: Confirmation, Holy Matrimony, Unction of the sick and dying, Holy Orders and Penance, in addition, of course, to Baptism and the Holy Communion. This venerable reckoning has the advantage of corresponding to the great crises and needs of human life-birth (Baptism); adolescence (Confirmation); marriage (Holy Matrimony); authorized leadership (Holy Orders); cleansing (Penance); sustenance (Holy Communion); sickness and death (Unction). Whether they are to be reckoned strictly as sacraments, the truth is that all of them are used in the Episcopal Church.*

No part of the 1979 prayer book caused more discussion and resulted in more of a compromise than the question of Confirmation. Basing their views on the practice of the early Christian church the revisers originally proposed to make Confirmation simply a part of the baptismal liturgy. This had been suitable in the early church, where almost all baptisms were those of adults, but when infants began to be baptized it was judged desirable to add another sacramental rite to baptism—sometimes it was said to be "completing baptism"—which was called "Confirmation." In the 1928 prayer book the liturgy's full title was: "The Order of Confirmation or Laying on of Hands upon Those that are Baptized." At the conclusion of the liturgy this rubric was added: "And there shall none be admitted to the Holy Communion, until such time as he be confirmed, or be ready and desirous to be confirmed." This omission in 1979 raised a very considerable opposition, especially in

---

* Because the Episcopal Church's views on the ministry are set forth elsewhere, Holy Orders is not discussed in this chapter.

the House of Bishops, and it was clear that a compromise was going to be required. The original revisers won one important point—baptism entitles any baptized person to receive the Holy Communion at any age. The Catechism, as it was revised for the 1979 prayer book, says this about baptism: "[It] is the sacrament by which God adopts us as his children and *makes us members of Christ's Body, the Church.*" However, in the introductory rubric to the liturgy for Confirmation these words appear: "In the course of their Christian development, those baptized at an early age are expected, when they are ready and have been duly prepared, to make a mature public affirmation of their faith and commitment to the responsibilities of their Baptism and to receive the laying on of hands by the bishop."

This process might be compared to the civil status of a child born in the United States. By virtue of that birth such a child is a fully recognized citizen of this nation. However, some of the privileges of citizenship are reserved until a later time. Voting in an election or serving on a jury has an age set at which such an exercise of responsibility is deemed to be appropriate. So a baptized person of any age is considered a member of the church, including the privilege of sharing in the Holy Communion. But to exercise all the responsibilities of membership obviously requires a mature and adult decision. Confirmation does not make one a member of the church. It does welcome a baptized member into the responsibilities of church life and Christ's mission to the world.

Whether marriage is to be counted strictly as a sacrament may be doubted on the grounds that it was not "instituted of Christ," but that it is sacramental in its character, that it employs a physical relationship to teach deep meanings of mutuality and love, and even to symbolize the care and concern which Christ has for the church, is undeniably the teaching of the Bible and of 2000 years of Christian tradition. Because the Episcopal Church holds this high estimation of the marriage state, it believes that marriage must be life-long. To grow together in mutual understanding and self-giving requires a lifetime of disciplined care and thoughtfulness which rests not upon the varying tides of emotion but upon a steady determination of the whole heart and mind and will. Our sentimental and romantic views of love—largely dependent upon Hollywood and romantic novels— is directly challenged by the prayer book's marriage rite. The language of that rite requires the bride and the groom to promise "to love and to cherish, until we are parted by death." Love is a matter of decision, of promise, of determination—not only a matter of emotion and feeling and impulse. Men and women are drawn to one another by those things; in marriage they promise to transform this initial attraction into a union and mutuality described by our Lord as being made "one flesh."

Unhappily, not all the relationships which are

called marriages begin with this determination, and of those that do, many come to grief against the hard and stubborn facts of human self-assertiveness and pride and willfulness. Our Lord once admitted that because of "the hardness of men's hearts" the ideal of marriage is sometimes frustrated. What shall the church do in such cases? They are the trial of every conscientious Episcopal clergyman. He will feel deep sympathy with a couple, one or both of whom for one reason or another have terminated legally their marriage to another partner and now desire to start again and rescue the experience of married love in another relationship. Indeed, in some cases the clergyman will even have counseled a divorce and will advise the desirability of another marriage. What can the church do? It cannot lightly allow its service to be repeated again, for what meaning could then be given to the solemn words "until we are parted by death"?

In some cases it may be determined that the past circumstances and present intentions and promises of the couple justify the church in marrying them despite a previous marital failure, and this may be done with the bishop's advice and consent. Sometimes this course of action does not seem appropriate to the priest or to the bishop. What the church seeks to do is two things: first, to provide a strong witness to the world of the church's ideal of marriage as a life-long union of man and woman and, second, to manifest a pastoral sympathy for those who because of "the hardness of men's hearts" have not been able to fulfill one of the conditions of that ideal. This may satisfy neither the rigorist who would exclude such people from communion and church fellowship forever afterward, nor the liberal who would remarry them again without heeding the possibility of scandal and offense to the church's ideal and a debasing of the principle of marital fidelity. As in so many things the Episcopal Church has found itself in a "middle way"—logically difficult to defend and maintain, but found in experience to correspond to the anomalies and paradoxes of life itself.

Even more important than the church's way of dealing with marriage failures is the church's way of seeking to avoid such failures as far as possible. The parish priest must give instruction on the nature of Christian marriage as one of his chief responsibilities. Any couple seeking to be married must receive such instruction and must notify the priest thirty days at least before the proposed ceremony so that he may arrange such preparation. In cases of marital discord the canon law requires the couple to report the discord to the minister if it threatens to destroy the marriage so that the minister may labor for a reconciliation. Many couples have testified that in the difficulties of their marriage—and what marriage does not have some such rocks and pitfalls—nothing was more helpful than the experience of going together to the Holy Communion, confessing together their failures and shortcomings, hearing the assurance of absolution, and receiving the Body and Blood of the loving and self-giving Christ in pardon and in renewal of life. This is one of the reasons why the church requires that the couple intend to take seriously their religious obligations and to make worship and prayer a part of their lives as a couple and a family. This is reflected in the rule that at least one of the partners must be a baptized Christian.

Penance came to be associated in the medieval church with the practice of auricular confession to the priest. Aware of the dangers of this system as a general requirement—dangers of pettiness and over-scrupulosity—the Anglican Reformation did away with the requirement and for the average circum-stances prescribed instead a "General Confession" to be said together with the rest of the congregation and a general absolution to be said by the priest to the people "being penitent." This assumed that most people most of the time know something of the mean-ing of the power of sin in their own lives—or can be assisted to that knowledge by sermons, Bible read-ing, self-examination—and are able to acknowledge the sin in their hearts and to seek God's forgiveness. More than four hundred years of Anglicanism proves that assumption to be sound.

There is, however, always the possibility of ex-ceptions, of people who are perplexed in conscience, who need not just general exhortation, general con-fession, and general absolution but a more particu-lar treatment of a special problem. Episcopalians differ as to their belief about the frequency with which such instances occur. Some Anglo-Catholic priests assume that they occur fairly frequently and urge their people to make use on a regular basis of an adaptation of the traditional form of the Sacrament of Penance. Many Episcopalians, perhaps a majority on the other hand, find such instances rare. Of course, every Episcopal priest is prepared to hear a private confession. No Episcopal priest is at liberty to require such a private confession as a prerequisite for admission to the Holy Communion. This arrangement seems to me to be another instance of the extraordinary wisdom and understanding of human nature—both of its weaknesses and of its possibilities—which at so many points marks the Anglican Communion and the Episcopal Church.

The practice of Unction came to be reserved for cases in which death was regarded as imminent. As such, it was eliminated at the Reformation and only recently and with a new meaning—or perhaps we should say a recovery of its New Testament meaning and its usage in the primitive church—has once again found its way into the prayer book. It is now regarded as a legitimate part of the church's ministry to the sick, and far from being reserved for use in cases where death is imminent, expresses in its present form the purpose of healing and restoration. The prayers that follow refer to "the healing power of his love" and ask forgiveness of sins, release from suffering, and restoration to wholeness and strength.

It was perhaps inevitable that as a church committed to the sacramental principle the Episcopal Church should be one of the leaders in the revival among the traditional churches of the ministry of healing. Episcopalians should be familiar with psychosomatic analysis of disease, because of the use of the sacraments. Of course, one's mind and body and spirit are all intimately related, and the disorders of one aspect of one's personality are reflected in the whole personality. In this sense, a bodily healing may be regarded—as the New Testament regards it in many instances—as a sign of the coming of the kingdom of God, as a sign that faith and self-forgetfulness have put to flight the power of fear and anxiety and self-assertiveness. What is not justified, of course, is any view that sickness is always curable provided only that enough faith be brought to bear on the situation. Death is abolished only at the Resurrection of the dead. Mysterious as it may be, death is a universal experience, and sickness and infirmity is a reminder of that inescapable destiny. Fortunately, any healing movement in the Episcopal Church is set in the context of the prayer book in its totality, which helps to insure against faddist and one-sided misunderstandings of the real Christian attitude toward disease and death. I confess that I have had a devout Episcopalian tell me with great pride that she had never allowed herself to be examined by a physician and that she never would, because she believed that God could heal her. I wondered why on the same theory she bothered to eat or go to a dentist, but the pressures of time made a coward of me and I kept my wonderings to myself. A sacramental view of life will gratefully accept all that the physician can discover and can prescribe as a means of achieving health and vigor for the tasks of life. Surely the greatest ministry of healing the Episcopal Church performs is through the services of her doctors and nurses and in her church-operated hospitals and convalescent homes. That God can and does work also through the ministrations of a priest, who by assuring the sick person forgiveness of any sins that may have been committed and of a new status as God's child can release new impulses in him for health and soundness, is the basis for the church's ministry of spiritual healing. Every priest can testify to the wonders it has wrought.

Although it is not a sacrament, the Episcopal Church's ministry at the time of death is one of its great glories. A college professor told me once that although he never came to church it was a comfort to know that when he died he would have such a dignified and straightforward and moving burial service. Perhaps the Episcopal Church has over-sold itself! The majestic and yet simple atmosphere of the burial service is one way in which many people know the Episcopal Church who know it in no other way. Perhaps it will in time lead some of them to inquire further about a church that treats the solemn fact of death with such restraint, such profundity, and such realism. There is no conspiracy to hide the facts. Death has reached into the human community and left a gaping hole in its fabric. That fact is faced in all seriousness and solemnity. It is not just that someone has "gone through a door" or "passed away" (whatever that means) or "gone away for a while." "The Lord gave and the Lord hath taken away" is the simple and stark fact, as the prayer book sees it. In the committal the minister is directed to say: "Earth to earth, ashes to ashes, dust to dust." It is curious in an age which has made so much of realism that this honesty should be almost too much to face, and that many people should gladly welcome the attempts of some funeral directors and cemeteries (significantly renamed "memorial parks") to gloss over the realities. The fact of death, however, is faced under the perspective of God's fatherly care, our Lord's death and resurrection, the conviction that individuals have an eternal significance precisely in their individuality as that individuality finds expression in trust and in love. There is therefore no extravagant rehearsal of the virtues of the deceased, a fact that insures the essential democracy of the service. How false many eulogies must seem in God's eyes—some saying too much, some too little. Only God who knows the secrets of the heart can deliver an adequate eulogy, and so the Episcopal service is content to remind us that he cares, that in Christ he forgives, that he receives and fulfills beyond our comprehension or understanding. When it has said that and prayed for that upon the deceased and upon those who mourn and upon us all who are made aware once again of the brevity and vanity of life apart from the Christian faith—then the church is content to carry the body to its resting place and commit it "in sure and certain hope of the Resurrection to eternal life," and the service is concluded.

I cannot imagine my Christian life apart from the sacramental life of the Episcopal Church, its ability to uncover in all the great experiences of life something of God's grace and God's purpose and God's power, its use of the things of sense—water, bread and wine, the human hand—to convey the reality of that which is unseen but by which men live out their existence and set their course. The sacraments, as St. Irenaeus said in the second century, "proclaim harmoniously the unity of flesh and spirit." What an incalculable effect that idea has had in western culture and civilization! Because it has made God real to me as the ground and source and meaning of every aspect of existence, I am forever grateful for the sacramental life of the Episcopal Church.

Four

Beauty To Behold

The first Episcopal church I ever stepped into would not be rated by any competent architect as an outstanding example of ecclesiastical art and architecture. It was a modest little frame building, without any stained glass windows, with a very much overcrowded chancel and sanctuary. And yet this modest building was the setting for my first real experience of a service of Christian worship which attempted to enlist every human art for the greater glory of God. An air of mystery and reverence permeated it. It was obviously not a building in which one engaged in idle conversation nor indeed in which the interests or ordinary ways of human beings were central. Attention focused upon the altar and the cross which stood in the midst of it. All of this struck me forcibly even in the unprepossessing little redwood church where I first shared in Anglican worship.

I did not know, of course, the long historical background of this atmosphere and attitude. Only in my later studies did the story unfold of how Anglicanism determinedly held on to the rich tradition of the use of the human arts in worship against the zeal of Puritan reformers. The Puritans, of course, had much logic on their side. They insisted that since the Reformation represented a drastic overhauling of the medieval theology and a return to the original religion of the New Testament, so the outward life of the church ought to symbolize this sharp discontinuity by a ruthless exclusion of anything reminiscent of the ways of worship in the past.

A large majority of the bishops of the Elizabethan church shared this point of view. The influence of Queen Elizabeth was almost surely felt here and at some other points in the English Reformation. In fact, she failed only once on what was to her an important point—the celibacy of the clergy. Perhaps it soothed her troubled conscience that at least "The Supreme Governor" of the Church of England—as she styled herself—never married! Richard Cox, made Bishop of Ely by Elizabeth I, wrote, for example, to one of his friends on the continent, "We are . . . constrained to our great distress of mind, to tolerate in our churches the image of the Cross and him who was crucified: the Lord must be entreated that this stumbling block may at length be removed." Cox was referring to Elizabeth's insistence that the crucifix be retained in the churches, and although the opposition of most of the bishops persuaded her to withdraw from this position, she was not so easily moved on other similar issues. One of the Royal Injunctions of 1559 provided that the clergy were to be appareled as in the last year of Edward VI. The bishops were greatly disturbed at this provision, for, as one of them wrote, "We are not ignorant what occasion the Papists will take from thence, as a cause of stumbling to the weak . . . Retaining the outward habits and inward feeling of popery, so fascinates the ears and eyes of the multitude, that they are unable to believe, but that either the Popish doctrine is still retained or at least that it will shortly be restored." On this matter, however, the Queen was adamant. Her reasons were presumably practical; she sought to establish customs of church life which would reassure the average English Christian that the Church of England was the same church that his or her ancestors had known and that Reformation did not mean an absolute break with the past. Such temporizing struck the Puritan-minded clergy as unworthy and dangerous. Although their protests continued, and actually forced some slight modification of the enforcement of the royal injunction, Elizabeth won the day.

The whole discussion, although it centered on a relatively minor point of the use of certain kinds of vestments, was nevertheless symbolic of a determination of Anglicanism which has continued to the present day. If one wants to measure the difference between the way in which Anglicanism retained its continuity with its past and the way in which Calvinism consciously sought to disrupt that continuity, let him consider the contrast between Westminster Abbey in London and another great church dedicated to St. Pierre, the Cathedral in Geneva. In the Abbey in London the past is gratefully accepted and helps to mold and fashion contemporary Christian life and worship. The altar, richly hung and ornamented, occupies its traditional place in the east end of the chancel. Rich wood carving ornaments the choir stalls, candles gleam, and choir and clergy are vested in ways that carry the imagination back for a thousand years. St. Pierre's Cathedral in Geneva, while it has its own peculiar dignity, bears a very different aspect. Where the altar once stood, rows of unornamented benches provide space for an unvested choir. Although a plain table stands in front of this choir section, the obvious focus of attention is a large pulpit which stands on the left, well down into the nave of the cathedral. No candles, rich embroidery, or ornamental woodwork soften the austerities of this building's interior, although some stained glass has made its appearance in the windows. No one will suggest that this setting for worship is without its own power and dignity, but it is bare and cold beside the warmth and richness of Westminster Abbey. In seeing these two churches I learned as I had never known before the meaning of the Anglican tradition.

The full richness of Anglican worship, of course, is not to be found in every village and hamlet. There are fearful and wonderful examples of poor taste in many Episcopal churches that one could mention, but the overall impression that one gains as he goes about the country is that again and again the Episcopal Church in a community, simple and modest as may be its proportions and adornment, breathes an atmosphere of God-centered worship that is not suggested by many other protestant churches in its neighborhood. The art and architecture of Anglicanism has been affected by theological movements and controversies. On the whole, however, the decorative and architectural features of Episcopal Church buildings described here apply to a majority of the churches one will encounter. Most Episcopal churches focus the attention of the visitor at once upon the altar, the setting for the celebration of the sacrament of the Holy Communion which has become more and more the center and norm of the church's worship. On or near most altars a cross is to be found, reminiscent of St. Paul's determination that Christ and him crucified must be the center of any genuine Christian faith and life. Usually candles stand upon the altar, carrying the worshiper in imagination back to the times when this was the only source of illumination. Time and tradition, however, have invested these candles with symbolic significance, two candles being representative of the divine and the human natures of our Lord, seven-branch candelabra reminding us of the ancient Hebrew number which symbolized the perfection of heaven. But perhaps the most eloquent suggestion of the symbolism of candles is that mentioned in the Royal Injunction of 1547, that two lights should be placed upon the altar "to signify the joy and splendor we receive from the light of Christ's blessed Gospel."

Centuries-old tradition governs the ornamentation of the altar. The English tradition calls for a richly ornamented "frontal," which covers the full length and height of the altar, oftentimes in the appropriate color for the season of the church year and ornamented by embroidered symbols. More frequent perhaps in American Episcopal churches is what is called the "superfrontal," a covering which hangs down for about a foot over the front of the altar, and also bears symbolic embroidery against the background of the season color. A fair linen cloth covers the top of the altar and hangs down, generously on both sides; this cloth bears five embroidered crosses, symbolizing the five wounds in the body of the crucified Christ. Forming the background for the altar, there will be perhaps a carved wood or stone reredos or a curtain, called a "dossal," either a permanent hanging or one which represents the seasonal colors and is changed correspondingly. Sometimes at right angles from the back wall stand two rods from which hang curtains which enclose the altar on either side. These are called "riddels." The altar, thus surrounded on three sides by curtains, is reminiscent of the Temple altar of Judaism, which was, however, completely surrounded by hangings to hide it from the eyes of the worshipers. The altar area, called the sanctuary, is generally divided from the rest of the chancel by rails, and custom discourages persons who have no part in the service at the altar from entering within these rails.

Both pulpit and lectern are placed to one side so that for the majority of the congregation sitting in the nave the view of the altar is not interfered with. The font, in which baptisms are performed, is often placed near the door of the church, symbolizing the fact that it is by Baptism that entrance and admission into the church takes place. Oftentimes, the church is designed in a cruciform manner, the arms of the design being supplied by transepts, the head of the cross design being the choir and sanctuary, and the long vertical line being supplied by the nave. Although this traditional pattern is found in an overwhelming number of Episcopal churches, architectural experimentation has also found a ready response from Episcopal congregations. New interest in the liturgy and in public worship as an expression of the essential social philosophy of the Christian faith has resulted in some new designs which place the altar in the center of the building so that the majority of the congregation may have the most direct view of it and access to it. Whatever new experiments are made, however, they will reflect the long Anglican tradition which regards all the arts of mankind as useful aids to worship and as legitimate offerings to the glory of God.

Clerical vestments, once one of the thorny problems of Elizabethan Anglicanism, are now universally accepted and valued in the Episcopal Church, both as a way of symbolizing the distinctive ministry of the clergy in preaching and worship and as testifying to the long history of Christian devotion, reaching back nearly 2000 years. The vestments which are used in many Episcopal churches, for example, at the celebration of the Holy Communion, are directly reminiscent of the customary dress of the Roman citizen of 150 A.D. The customary vestments for the choir offices (that is, Morning and Evening Prayer, because they are read in the choir area of the church and not behind the altar rails) do not have as long a history, but the academic hoods and tippets may remind the worshiper of the age-old alliance between religion and learning and conjure up visions of monastic worship where a hood and a fur-lined tippet were necessities in a drafty and unheated medieval chapel.

The retention of these traditional vestments is sometimes criticized for the reason that they suggest a sharp separation between clergy and laity and also because they seem to make Christianity so much a thing of the past. Is there not a certain unreality about "dressing up" to look like Roman citizens of the second century A.D. and does it not make the clergy seem sharply separated and quite remote from the workaday world of the laity? These objections, of course, have some weight, but they might equally be pressed against the custom of academic dress at solemn functions of the modern college or university. Although religion does have contemporary relevance if it is to be treated seriously at all, Christianity as well as Judaism is an historical faith. It looks to the past; it calls to remembrance what God has done in history. It insists that the Holy Spirit has taught and led people through the experiences of two thousand years into much wisdom and insight. The Christian religion is not something that the modern worshiper is free to render as he likes. Although in one important sense, each worshiper must make the Christian faith his own, in another sense it is not his own at all but is an historic faith, maintained at great cost, wise and rich with the accumulated experience of the centuries, claiming our attention today precisely because it has interpreted and clarified life through such a long past. To go into an Episcopal church and to take part in an Episcopal service of worship makes all this eloquently apparent. The modern worshiper sees himself at once in proper perspective. Here is something, obviously, that has been going on for a long time before I arrived on the scene and presumably will continue for a long time after I have left it. It is something to which I, of course, may make a fresh and creative contribution, but it is first of all something which the labors and witness of others have handed on to me. My first obligation is to understand it in all its historical richness, and then I shall perhaps be enabled to add something of my own to this incredibly rich deposit. Someone has said that the trouble with much modern Christianity is that it has "failed to read the minutes of the previous meetings." By the outward aspect of its worship, the Episcopal Church does much to correct this oversight.

The worship in an Episcopal Church is not only rich in historical reminiscence; it is also surprisingly wise in its psychological insights. The outsider may complain that to worship as an Episcopalian is an extraordinarily strenuous undertaking! Kneeling, sitting down, getting up, bowing—all of this, as well as continually trying to find one's way through a prayer book, is a surprising way to worship for one who is accustomed to sitting in a pew and simply listening to what's going on. The Episcopal Church, however, is making use in these traditional postures of worship of a psychological insight which is ages old in its use but only recently has had experimental verification. The emotion, says psychology, often follows the action. It is not only true that one runs away because he is afraid; it is also true that the act of running away augments the fear. The proposal of the heroine in the Rodgers and Hammerstein musical comedy, *The King and I,* that suggests the strategy of "whistling a happy tune" whenever one is afraid, is a sound psychological device. The Episcopal Church is aware that human emotion is a very undependable thing indeed. One's moods are often sluggish and earthbound and stubbornly resistant to the soaring and lifting themes of Christian adoration and worship. It helps, however, to do something to express this mood which the church would instill. Just the simple act of kneeling when one comes into a

church, a custom of most Episcopalians, will h
turn the thoughts and mood of the worshiper towaiu
God and to lift him above the level of his own immediate anxieties and ambitions. To sit down to listen
to a lesson from the Bible, and then to stand to join in
a great hymn of adoration such as the Te Deum, does
not necessarily mean, of course, that one will be at-
tentive to the lesson nor that his spirit will rise auto-
matically in ecstatic adoration to match the ancient
hymn of praise. The posture and the gesture, however, do help to create the mood and the attitude.
What is more, of course, the very experience of watch-
ing others actively participating in worship in these
ways helps to overcome one's own sluggishness and
to quicken his sensitivity to the reality of God and
the way in which he touches and helps human life.

Some newcomers are baffled by the seeming variety, however, of these ceremonial usages which they
find practiced both by the clergy and the congregation. They feel that as newcomers they will be conspicuous by their failure to do what others are doing
at the right place and in the right way. It will help to
reassure such people to remind them that many Episcopalians are as baffled as they are by some things
they see. As a matter of fact, almost anything one does
will probably be considered—no matter how bizarre
it may be—as some newfangled practice which is the
norm somewhere or other! Many of the widespread
customs have very dubious historical justification
anyway, and some of them are developed by purists

and scholars of the history of church ceremonial. My advice to the newcomer is that if he misses some piece of action in the service in which the rest of the congregation takes part, he assume an air of superior knowledge, which will suggest to the others in the congregation that he is privy to some secret of ceremonial scholarship of which they in their ignorance are still not aware! From the days of the first prayer book of Edward VI (1549) there has been a wide toleration of all kinds of ceremonial practices, a tolerance that finds expression in the quaint language of that prayer book: "As touching, kneeling, crossing, holding up of hands, knocking upon the breast, and other gestures: they may be used or left as every man's devotion serveth without blame." One may worship in an Episcopal church with the barest kind of simplicity and the prayer book may be read without any embellishments of ceremonial except those which are required by the rubrics of the service itself. On the other hand, an Episcopal church in the next town, or only a few blocks away, will surround the reading of a service with the most elaborate action and pageantry, complete with incense, bowing, the sign of the cross, holy water, and many other things with which the ordinary protestant is completely unfamiliar.

This liberty in what everyone agrees are non-essentials of Christian worship has, of course, been found in the church throughout its history. Differences between the usages of the church at Rome, the church in Gaul, the church in Britain, and elsewhere—this variety has always obtained and as long as people differ in taste and outlook it presumably will always continue. If Christians are ever to achieve the reunion of the separated churches, which we discuss elsewhere in this book, it can only be by the adoption of some such broad and liberal policy concerning public worship which has been a mark of the Anglican tradition. There must be room, for example, for the kind of public worship that celebrates the glory and wonder of God's being and purpose in pageantry and ceremonial which makes use of all his gifts in expressing our adoration of him.

It was my privilege for many years to live near the great Cathedral of St. John the Divine in New York City. Here the familiar services of the prayer book take on new significance, set against the background of a building of breathtaking proportions and boldness of design. The great high points of the Christian year are celebrated before vast congregations and with dramatic ceremonial which symbolizes the majesty and glory of the God whom we worship. On the other hand, I have had a very different but equally satisfying experience of worship in a simple rural mission in Virginia, where without the aid of great vistas of Gothic arches or the thrilling peal of a great organ or the unearthly beauty and purity of a highly trained boys' choir we have simply read the majestic words of the prayer book, and felt the warmth and intimacy of God's concern with every individual and the sense of his presence wherever two or three are gathered together in his name.

The Episcopal Church's worship as it is now prescribed and carried on is not, of course, a model which the ecumenical church in the future can take over without amendment and enrichment. For example, the Quaker experience of the power and reality of the ministry of silence is not sufficiently provided for in the present formula of Anglican worship. Indeed, there often seems to be a kind of conspiracy between the clergy and the organist to fill in even the few moments of necessary silence with some kind of music so that there is always "something going on." Especially in recent revisions of the prayer book—more flexibility and more optional usages are encouraged, pointing the way toward the kind of variety which will have to characterize any ecumenical or universal church if it is really to comprehend all the diversified tastes and temperaments that go to make up the human family. By its use of beauty, color, the art and craftsmanship of the human race, precious metals, movement and pageantry, the Episcopal Church speaks eloquently of a God who sanctifies the best and highest aspirations and achievements of the human spirit, accepting and using all that we have to offer him, and blessing and converting mankind thereby. It was this instinct in the Episcopal Church that commended her to me from our first acquaintance and which continues to inspire and delight me as I live and worship in her tradition.

Five

Membership

As early as my confirmation class I found the Episcopal Church to be extraordinarily liberal and broad in its appreciation of the role of man's intellect and reason in his Christian life. It was the mid-twenties, and the Fundamentalist-Modernist controversy was raging everywhere. I was not a very well-informed or passionate rebel—but I was rebellious, with the awe-inspiring conviction of the young that my own opinions were of inestimable importance. To my great relief the theological requirements of the Episcopal Church as they were presented to me in that confirmation class were minimal and had to do with basic affirmations of belief. Somehow the recitation of the Apostles' or the Nicene Creed in public worship with the rest of the congregation did not disturb me very much—although I personally would have preferred some editing of specific phrases. I did not learn until much later of the form in which the Nicene Creed is repeated among the Eastern Orthodox Christians, which usage has now been recovered in the prayer book: *"We* believe . . ." Even though I was obliged to repeat the creed in the first person singular in the 1928 prayer book, I did so in the company of the whole congregation, and this somehow took much of the burden of personal comprehension and conviction off my shoulders. The creeds were like the Pledge of Allegiance to the Flag—a statement of the platform of this society and community. I was willing to accept it as such even though I continued to have some minor difficulties with specific phrases. Of which more later. I still would say to the doubter or the inquirer who finds the creed a stumbling block, "Do you believe the main thing—that God is in Christ offering us his love and his pardon? If so, trust the church's wisdom for the detailed way that fundamental faith has been expressed. This was her faith before it was yours. Some day you may see it her way."

I was greatly relieved intellectually when the rector in a casual remark to the confirmation class observed that as long as one was able to say "I believe in God the Father, Creator of heaven and earth," he was perfectly free to accept any version of the manner in which the creation was accomplished which science suggested to be true. The sanity and wisdom of this approach to the Bible appealed to me greatly. I did not know then what I know now, namely that behind this casual remark in confirmation class lay a long history of Anglicanism with its distinctive understanding of the role of scripture in Christian thought and life. Because this history has had much to do with freeing the Anglican from the bitterness of the controversy over the Bible that has raged in other Christian circles, perhaps it deserves some brief summary here.

The great Anglican theologian, Richard Hooker, writing toward the end of the reign of Queen Elizabeth I, was confronted in the Puritan movement with a totalitarian and authoritarian understanding of the scriptures and their place in the Christian church. Under the leadership of Thomas Cartwright, Lady Margaret Professor of Divinity at Cambridge University, the Puritan movement had taken the position that even in the details of her worship and governmental organization the church was bound to strict obedience to the laws of God as revealed in the Bible. Hooker's *Laws of Ecclesiastical Polity* attacked this contention by insisting that the Bible was not the only place where God's laws could be discovered. God also makes his laws known to us through our reason, operating on the evidence of our senses and of history. The Bible has as its single task, according to Hooker, the declaration of the saving purpose of God in Christ and the necessity for trusting in him as the center and ground of Christian discipleship.

To make clear this crucial Christian revelation, the Bible is for Hooker all-important and all-sufficient. A wide range of questions, however, find no conclusive answer in scripture at all. Some of these questions are practical ones, having to do with the relation of the church to the state, the internal government of the church, the ceremonial embellishment of the church's worship, and many others. Some are of a theological character. For example, the nature of the presence of Christ in the Holy Communion is regarded by Hooker as a matter on which the Bible does not speak definitively, at least not in detail about its mode or manner. A whole range of questions on which the Bible throws no direct light are primarily cultural or intellectual in character: the nature and processes of the physical world, the constitution and functioning of human society, the whole cultural and historical development of mankind. As one thinks about these questions, using his faculties of observation and reason, he is in a very real sense, according to Hooker, discovering some of the laws of God.

The result of this repudiation of the exclusive role of the Bible as the only guide for the Christian meant that Anglicanism was prepared to assign enormous importance to man's cultural and intellectual activities. This reflected itself in the encouragement given to the growth and development of the two great English universities, Cambridge and Oxford. Both of them took seriously the obligations of churchmanship and yet left free the ranging curiosity of the human intellect, believing that no honest and conscientious use of the mind will disclose anything but further truth about God. As a result of this tradition, which might be called "Christian humanism," the English village vicar has often combined with his spiritual duties some intellectual hobby which may, as a matter of fact, qualify him as something of an expert in his particular field of interest and study. Whatever disadvantages this breadth of interest has involved—and it must be confessed that it has sometimes meant a kind of ivory tower academic seclusion from the practical concerns of the laity of the church—it has meant nevertheless that Anglicanism has been one of the most congenial spiritual homes for men and women of broad intellectual interests and sympathies.

Admittedly, there continues to be controversy about the role of the Bible in the life of the church. One sometimes hears it said—when a church convention or the House of Bishops or just an individual priest or theology professor makes a statement about the Christian implications of some social or moral issue in our national life or the life of the world—"Jesus never said anything about that." Hooker's answer would have been that there are other aids to the search for Christian truth besides the words of Jesus in the Bible. Jesus foresaw the fact that the world would change or as one of our hymns puts it, "new occasions teach new duties." St. John's Gospel (16:12-13) has the Lord say "I have much more to tell you, but now it would be too much for you to bear. When, however, the Spirit comes he will lead you into all the truth . . . He will give me glory, because he will take what I say and tell it to you." In the light of that saying the church decided to admit non-Jews into its membership, to call for the abolition of slavery, and to ordain women, and made other decisions about which the Lord in his earthly life was silent.

In theology, this broad platform of intellectual interest has meant a wider and keener interest in historical theology than has been characteristic of most other Christian churches. The Anglican theologian is not content with the exposition of some biblical text. He will insist on bringing to bear also the wisdom and insights of the church Fathers. In the beginning of the Reformation this wide interest in the church's great theological tradition—especially its pre-medieval version—was characteristic of almost all the leading protestant thinkers. The great Elizabethan divine, John Jewel, corresponded regularly with his friends in the Swiss churches, and the correspondence was filled with learned references to Cyprian, Augustine, Ambrose, and the other worthies of the Patristic period. As protestantism developed, however, it became the distinctive hallmark of Anglicanism to be concerned with the long and rich tradition of Christian thought. Perhaps this sometimes resulted in a lack of careful attention to the analysis of biblical themes and texts. The Scotch Presbyterian or the continental protestant was often more illuminating in his treatment of the Bible than was his Anglican counterpart. On the other hand, his Anglican counterpart was often broader and more inclusive in his concerns with human life and human history.

At least one notable advantage of the Anglican approach and treatment of theology appeared in the crisis over higher criticism of the Bible which broke over the Christian church in the 19th and early 20th centuries. Like any other group of people, Anglicanism in general and the Episcopal Church in America in particular, had its full quota of conservatives—perhaps a little more than its full quota—and there was a widespread sense of shock and dismay at the implications of the new discoveries about the ways in which the Bible had been written and given its present form. It is notable, however, that at least in America the so-called Fundamentalist Movement probably had less success and importance in the Episcopal Church than in any other major protestant body. Since the Anglican ethos had always emphasized the authority of the church and of its age-long tradition as the interpreters of scripture, the discovery that wholly new modes of interpretation of scripture were required by the discoveries of the higher critics dismayed Anglicans less than many other protestants. Familiarity with the Church Fathers, for example, had already taught Anglicans that there was more than one way to read the Bible and more than one sense in which any given passage might be taken. The wide use of allegory, for example, suggested that Christians in different periods of the church's history might use scripture in quite different ways. What was more obvious than that in our time scripture would have to be read with new methods of interpretation?

The use of the Apostles' and Nicene Creeds as the statements of faith in the Episcopal Book of Common Prayer had always served to give perspective to the Bible and to hold up for attention the great central story of God's dealings with man which the Bible represents. Without this guidance it would have been much easier for Anglicanism to fall into a kind of textual bibliolatry. To question the accuracy, for example, of the opening chapters of the Book of Genesis as an historical description of the ways in which the creation of the world came about would, of course, be initially a shock to a traditionally minded Episcopalian as much as to a member of any other of the main Christian traditions. But after the initial shock had passed, the Episcopalian might recall that one of the frequently used historic creeds had never said more than that God was ultimately responsible for bringing into being "all that is seen and unseen." If this is the main thing which we learn from the Book of Genesis, then perhaps it is not so crucial to believe that the process of creation took place in just exactly the manner in which it is there recounted. Growing up as I did in an age of widespread skepticism about the Bible, it was important beyond estimation to find that the Episcopal Church had long since laid hold of a few basic biblical themes as being central and important and that one could concentrate his spiritual and intellectual energies in the consideration of these great matters rather than undertaking the impossible task of defending every word of the Bible as infallibly and literally true.

The use of the historic creeds has, of course, posed some problems of conscience and scruple for modern men and women. The creeds admittedly employ what it is now fashionable to call "mythological" language. A cosmology in which God "comes down" from heaven, and "ascends" up into it again, and a conception of one of the Persons of the Triune God sitting "on the right hand" of the other, has troubled many modern people. Of course, this is a problem for any Christian church that regards the Bible as having any authority whatever in the establishment of doctrine. The important role given in Anglicanism to the use of reason leads, however, to a recognition of the essentially poetic and mythological character of such language.

Somewhat more difficult, however—at least for me—has been the inclusion of the reference to the Virgin Birth of our Lord in the creed. I am convinced that the true genius of Anglicanism requires us to treat this question as one of historical evidence and therefore to leave the way open for the individual Episcopalian to doubt it or affirm it as an historic fact, depending upon the way in which the evidence strikes each one. Scholars agree that the church put the phrase "born of the Virgin Mary" into the creed not primarily in order to insist upon the virginal conception of our Lord but rather to insist upon the fact that he had a human mother and was therefore fully a human being and also that his birth came about by

God's initiating activity. In other words, one may affirm what the church meant to teach by the reference to the Virgin Birth without making up his mind about its historical accuracy, a matter on which the evidence is by many Christian scholars now thought to be inconclusive. But not all Episcopalians—not even all Episcopalians who are scholars—will agree with me on this point.

This exhibition of differences within the Anglican community will, perhaps, teach the outsider something of the nature of our unity. Obviously no one can be an Episcopalian who does not share in language which assumes the validity of the Trinity and the Incarnation, and what those central doctrines teach and imply. What cannot, however, be required is any decision on what is essentially a matter of historical evidence, namely, the way in which the Incarnation took place in terms of specific historical events. That in Jesus Christ we see God come in the flesh is of the essence of the creeds and indeed of the New Testament itself. To dogmatize, however, on a matter where evidence must be determinative seems to me a very un-Anglican thing to do. To assure the reader that I speak here for a substantial number of Anglicans, I would refer him to a book issued some time ago in the Church of England which reports the following situation with respect to the attitude toward this question in that Mother Church of Anglicanism: "Many of us hold . . . that belief in the Word made flesh is integrally bound up with belief in the Virgin

Birth . . .; there are, however, some among us who hold that a full belief in the historical Incarnation is more consistent with the supposition that our Lord's birth took place under the normal conditions of human generation . . . We . . . recognize that both the views outlined . . . are held by members of the church . . . who fully accept the reality of our Lord's Incarnation, which is the central truth of the Christian faith."* The fact is that at the present time the theological situation in the Episcopal Church is marked both by an increasing agreement on the central issues of the Christian faith and by a continuing difference of opinion about just which affirmations are to be considered as central! Anglicanism is hesitant about premature dogmatism and prefers to leave questions such as these to be resolved by further study and prayer.

I was also attracted by the modesty of the claims of Anglican theology. It was obvious that here was no rigid theological blueprint, no attempt to "unscrew the inscrutable." The mystery and incomprehensibility of God was reflected in the church's lack of precision and definition at many points. I was impressed with the amount of reverent agnosticism that was permitted in this version of Christianity. Wide differences of points of view were obviously allowed on matters which had rent asunder other communions and church traditions. No single Christian

---

*Doctrine in the Church of England. Macmillan, New York, 1938. Page 82-83.

thinker dominated the Anglican theological scene. We were not called to believe in Hookerism or Cranmerism. Indeed it has always seemed to me that Anglicanism lacks any official theology. The Bible alone, illuminated by two thousand years of Christian thought, is the only theological platform to which the Episcopal Church is fully committed. It is true that the 39 Articles of Religion have had an authoritative position in Anglicanism since their formulation in the 16th century. However, an examination of the 39 Articles reveals that they are content simply to reiterate biblical themes and ideas, and indeed make the flat assertion that "Holy Scripture containeth all things necessary to salvation." The historic creeds themselves are justified in the 39 Articles only on the ground that "they may be proved by most certain warrants of Holy Scripture" (Article 8, Of the Creeds). The church's authority in interpreting scripture is affirmed (Article 20, Of the Authority of the Church: "The Church hath . . . authority in Controversies of Faith"). On the other hand this authority is plainly limited ("it is not lawful for the church to ordain anything that is contrary to God's Word written, neither may it so expound one place of scripture, that it be repugnant to another").

What is perhaps most striking about the 39 Articles is that in some of the deep matters of the Christian faith there is a parsimony of words and a modesty of theological ambition. The great biblical idea of election and predestination, for example, is treated in Article 17, but how different this Article is from the decisions of the famous Synod of Dort, a 17th century synod of the Dutch Reformed church reflecting an attempt to press the definition of God's sovereignty to the point of virtually eliminating man's freedom and responsibility. The Article on Predestination and Election follows closely the Christian experience of St. Paul as that is recorded in the Epistle to the Romans. All Christians know that they have been "called" into whatever Christian understanding or virtue they possess. Anyone who reflects at all about the course of his life knows how much of what has been precious and valuable has simply been given to him. Some of the most important relationships of my life came about not through my choice but through the intervention and gift of others. The Christian interprets these experiences as the guiding and leading of the providence of God. Why am I a Christian while my friend who is obviously intellectually and spiritually my superior is not? This was the real problem which confronted St. Paul, for example, and led him to his discussion of the doctrine of election and predestination. The only answer, I believe, is that God in his infinite wisdom and knowledge about the workings of the human will and mind has made known to me what he has not yet for some strange reason made known to my friend, namely, the unsearchable riches of Christ.

Article 17 says something very much like this and finds that "the godly consideration" of this fact of

ft of insight and power is the heart and mo-
f all Christian life. This is not a doctrine,
ever, to be thundered abroad to the unbeliever—
or, as the Article puts it, to "curious and carnal persons, lacking the spirit of Christ." In other words, to press the doctrine of election and predestination in such a way as to deny man's responsibility and freedom goes far beyond the meaning that the doctrine holds in the Bible itself. Likewise any interpretation of predestination which denies God's universal love for mankind—or as the Article puts it, "God's promises . . . as they be *generally* set forth in Holy Scripture"—is carefully guarded against. Such is the modesty of the Anglican treatment of one of the theological doctrines that has caused schisms and heartaches throughout wide areas of Christendom.

The result of this refusal to develop an official theology has been that Anglicanism has never suffered any major doctrinal schisms. The defection from the American Episcopal Church of a small group of clergy and laity in the mid-nineteenth century over the issue of baptismal regeneration proved to be numerically insignificant, and the resulting Reformed Episcopal Church has never spread far beyond a few of the larger cities of the eastern seaboard. Some minor schisms have taken place in recent years, but they appear also to represent only a small and insignificant number of Episcopalians. Outsiders find this breadth and tolerance difficult to believe, and one is often asked questions like: "Are you a High Church

Episcopalian or a Low Church Episcopalian?" Such a questioner often assumes that these differences are hard and fast ones, representing almost distinct branches within the Episcopal Church as a whole. Nothing, of course, could be farther from the truth. Very few dioceses and very few parishes are of a "monochrome" type, representing, that is, only one kind of theological slant. As a matter of fact, the very terms "Low Church" and "High Church" have had such a complicated development in meaning that their usefulness in describing even present tendencies within the thought and life of the Episcopal Church is highly questionable. The "High Churchman" of 1688, for example, is certainly not identical either in theology or in ceremonial with the Anglo-Catholic of the modern day. All that one can say is that there have been in the history of Anglicanism a variety of theological and ecclesiastical schools of thought and that today at least three such tendencies can be observed.

There is, in the first place, the Anglo-Catholic Movement. Its main interest is to stress both in its theology and ceremonial the continuity of the present-day church with the Holy Catholic Church in all the ages since our Lord's Resurrection and Ascension. In this stress and emphasis it has been conservative and historical, especially—by contrast with other tendencies in the Episcopal Church—with respect to the life and customs both of Eastern Orthodoxy and of the medieval Western Church. At the hands of a very small minority of its leaders it has sometimes seemed to take on an authoritarian rigidity which is, ironically enough, reminiscent most of all of the attitude of the Puritan party in the Elizabethan church. Like the Puritans of old, some few modern Anglo-Catholics, however, would rejoice in the diversity of the Anglican Communion, provided that such diversity did not tolerate departure from basic catholic doctrine. In many ways the Anglo-Catholic Movement within the Episcopal Church fulfills the function of a Conservative Party in a political spectrum. It is unwilling to see that which has behind it the weight of hundreds of years of tradition lightly cast aside. It reminds the religious worshiper that he is never "on his own" and that it is never quite true, as many like to claim, that anyone "has his own religion." Christianity is embedded in history, and the Anglo-Catholic Movement reminds us that, far from having "my own religion," we have a religion which has met and responded to all manner of situations and circumstances, has witnessed the rise and fall of empires, has ministered to men in their adversity as well as in their prosperity, has tamed and subdued civilizations and peoples and has stood steadfast and unbending under the bludgeoning of persecution. All Episcopalians, whether they call themselves Anglo-Catholics or not, show something of the marks of this great movement and tendency of thought in their religious attitude and outlook.

There is, in the second place, the Evangelical

Movement. Its main concern has been to emphasize the original Christian experience as it is recorded in the New Testament, recovered in the Protestant Reformation, proclaimed powerfully and eloquently in the Wesleyan Revival in England in the 18th and early 19th centuries, and vividly relevant today when men are once again asking deep questions of the meaning of their personal existence in a strangely hostile and threatening world. For the Evangelical, Christianity is primarily the personal acceptance of God's love in Christ as the ground and assurance of his forgiveness, acceptance, and status as a son of God. The favorite themes of Evangelical preaching are the devastating ruinous effects of sin in human life and the unbounded and overflowing love of God as evidenced in the life and death and resurrection of his Son. The great Christian succession, according to the Evangelical, runs from St. Paul through St. Augustine to Luther and Calvin to John Wesley and Charles Simeon and presently to modern Evangelicals. The Evangelical would remind his Anglo-Catholic brother that God is "able of these stones to raise up children unto Abraham" and that no trust can be put in anything less than God's forgiving and enabling love. The church is important but chiefly as the appointed means by which individual men and women are brought to accept their status as forgiven sinners, wholly dependent upon the mercy and grace of God. The presence of the Evangelical Movement in the Church of England is a sure witness to the fact that

Anglicanism shares fully in the tradition of the Protestant Reformation. The Anglo-Catholic Movement would stress the continuity of the Church of England with the catholic church in all ages; the Evangelical Movement would insist on the perennial necessity for judging the church's life by the supreme test of whether or not it is bearing witness to the unconditional love of God for penitent sinners.

Until a decade or two ago, many observers would have said that the Evangelical Movement was the weakest of the three schools of thought within Anglicanism, that it had conspicuously failed to win the allegiance and excite the interest of the younger clergy and that its power lay chiefly in some vested interests by which it continued to exert a disproportionate influence in the church. That all changed, I believe, with the rapid resurgence in English-speaking Christianity of what was called loosely "neo-orthodoxy." I myself found the position of this group of thinkers mightily persuasive in my seminary days, and I have found them so in many ways ever since, though new movements like "liberation theology" and the "theology of hope" have also modified the "neo-orthodoxy" of my youth and disturbed my tendency to theological complacency. Paul Tillich, Reinhold Nieburh, Karl Barth, Emil Brunner, and a hundred years ahead of them all, Søren Kierkegaard—a strange company of theological bedfellows to anyone who knows the details of their many sharp differences and even contradictions—

have all, however, made at least this single impact upon modern Christianity: they forced us to take seriously the full dimensions of the human problem of alienation, of lostness, of anxiety, of brokenness, of inner contradiction—or, to use an often misunderstood Christian word, "sin." None of the leaders is an Anglican, but then none of the chief Protestant Reformers was an Anglican either. True—there had to arise finally a Richard Hooker who could delineate a distinctively Anglican understanding of the Reformation theology. In our day, no such theological giant has made his appearance among us, and we are like the Church of England in the early years of the reign of Elizabeth I—dependent for our greatest theological stimulation on thinkers from outside our own fellowship. This very openness, this very humility, this very willingness to be taught by other communions and other traditions is an authentic part of the Anglican genius. We like to claim the adjective "moderate" and to speak of a "via media"—a middle way between two extremes. But in some periods of Anglicanism the initial impulse of thought that was "moderated" came from outside and had first to be fully felt and its validity largely accepted, and the "middle way" was between positions that were strongly represented by opposing schools of thought. There is no single Anglican theological position; there is only a distinctively Anglican theological method. I am glad to be a member of such a supple theological tradition which can now in our own time make large room for what contemporary protestant theology has to teach and tell us, even as it has room also for the best in Thomas Aquinas or Duns Scotus or, behind them, Augustine. The Evangelical school of thought in Anglicanism has had a genuine revival in our own generation.

More difficult to describe and to differentiate from the other two movements that have been mentioned above is the Broad Church or Liberal Movement in Anglicanism. Here the emphasis is on the continuity between man's religious life and interests and the rest of his existence. Drawing upon the insights of Hooker and, behind him, of the Renaissance tradition exemplified in Erasmus and John Colet, the emphasis of this school of thought has been upon the importance of man's reason and of its use in all manner of intellectual and cultural activities as a genuine part of his offering of himself to God. Broad Churchmen have been sympathetic to the social and intellectual developments of their time, seeking to identify the Christian church with all that is best and most hopeful in the contemporary society. This school of thought has had great influence in the Episcopal Church in America, and in recent years the involvement of the church in the struggles of ethnic and racial minorities for a fuller role in the decision-making process of the nation has become an accepted and established part of the church's program of ministry and witness, though not without widespread resistance and opposition. It is often not recognized what a long history lies behind this modern movement in Anglicanism. The responsibilities implied in the title "The Church of England" were interpreted by the Broad Churchmen of the 19th century to mean a concern that the church play a creative and formative role in the nation's total life. Not the church's continuity with its own past (the Anglo-Catholic concern) nor the church's foundation in a personal religious experience of forgiveness and new power for life (the Evangelical emphasis) but the role of the Christian church as expressing and consecrating all that is noblest and finest and most enlightened in human thinking and aspirations—this is the main stress of a Broad Churchman.

Obviously taken by itself each of these movements betrays some weaknesses. The Anglo-Catholic may become a rigid authoritarian; the Evangelical may become a sentimental individualist; the Broad Churchman may become an amiable reflection of the presuppositions of his immediate environment. Taken together, however, in a continuing encounter with each other, these three movements help to keep Anglicanism alive to the present, loyal to the past, and sensitive to man's utter dependence upon God's love and mercy. The late Archbishop of York, Dr. Cyril F. Garbett, in an address at the General Convention of the Episcopal Church in 1949, put it this way: "Anglicanism stands not for tolerance for the sake of compromise but for comprehension for the sake of truth." In a time when men are tempted to grasp for any easy religious reassurance, even one which involves the abdication of intellectual responsibility, and which turns away from the consideration of present-day human problems in an escape to some ivory-tower shrine of personal religious security, I am gladder than ever that I am an Episcopalian. I am glad that I belong to a tradition which is modest and reasonable in its approach to religious truth, that is many-sided and rich in its appreciation of the religious character of every aspect of man's existence, that is emphatic in its focus upon man's sin and God's love as the center of the Christian religion.

Six

Freedom and Authority

Every Episcopalian in his confirmation is made aware, by the presence and central responsibility of the bishop in the Confirmation service of the continuity of his own Christian life and that of the particular congregation to which he seeks to belong, with an authoritative tradition, reaching back to the days of the Apostles themselves. On the other hand, he soon discovers that he has been taken up into an extraordinarily democratic church organization where each man's voice can be heard and where the free processes of discussion, deliberation, and decision formulate major policy.

In some respects the polity of the Episcopal Church corresponds to the political situation in England. We find there, on the one hand, the greatest imaginable respect for democratic processes and for the freedom of the individual to speak his mind and to express his convictions. On the other hand, however, there is a deeply rooted respect for the Crown—

albeit vaguely defined—which gives continuity and stability to the national society. It would be misleading, of course, to suggest that the bishop is no more than a constitutional monarch, but the analogy is suggestive and illuminating. This unique combination of freedom and authority, representing a creative merging of ancient ecclesiastical tradition with modern political insight, is one of the important reasons why many people are drawn to the Episcopal Church and find it a most congenial spiritual home.

This combination of freedom and authority, of course, has its roots in the Bible itself. It is abundantly clear in the New Testament, for example, that freedom and liberty are essential and distinguishing marks of the Christian life. In the writing of St. Paul especially, one of the chief contrasts is between the new Israel, which is the Christian church, and the old Israel on this very matter of freedom and liberty. St. Paul frequently distinguishes the freedom and responsibility which the individual Christian enjoys in his relationship to God from the inhibited and enslaved kind of relationship which, he believed, was characteristic of Judaism. "For freedom Christ has set us free," he writes to the Galatians, "stand fast, therefore, and do not submit again to the yoke of slavery" (5:1). The use of the phrase "sons of God" establishes as the ideal of the Christian life a mature and responsible liberty. No Christianity which is consistent with the New Testament can set up as its ideal any kind of blind subservience or unquestioning obedience.

Although this point is made most clearly in the Pauline epistles, it must be noted that the whole manner and method of our Lord's ministry point in the same direction. It is a ministry of powerful effectiveness but marked by surprising reticence. No boastful claims are made about his special messianic character. Indeed, in St. Mark's Gospel, it is notable that he forbids any widespread publication of the success of his healing ministry, presumably on the grounds that he would not by such means coerce or beguile an awestruck and overwhelmed following. It has been pointed out also that the parables make great demands on the perception and insight of the individual. They may be taken simply as attractive and charming stories, and any man is free to hear them on that level alone. On the other hand, "he that hath ears to hear, let him hear." The man who would probe more deeply, seeking in these deceptively simple stories a clue to the meaning of life and the nature of God, will have his reward. Discipleship for Jesus was always a highly personal decision, involving oftentimes radical separation from one's tradition and background (hence the repetition of the injunction to leave father and mother, if necessary). Perhaps no other great religion of mankind makes as searching a demand and sets as high a value on the individual believer as does Christianity.

On the other hand, the New Testament is full of discussions of the concept of authority. It was one of the predominant notes of the ministry of Christ, and we read that "with authority commandeth he even the unclean spirits and they do obey him" (Luke 4:36). What is more, this same authority is bestowed upon his followers. "Then he called his twelve disciples together and gave them power and authority over all devils and to cure diseases. And he sent them to preach the kingdom of God and to heal the sick" (Luke 9:1 and 2). It has been pointed out that the same Greek word—*exousia*—can be translated both "authority" and also "power." That is to say, the New Testament recognizes that authority is always linked with effective power. We make the same connection in English when we speak, for example, of someone who plays the piano "with authority." This means that the pianist in question has a command of the techniques and possibilities of the instrument by reason of capacities and abilities. So authority in the New Testament is not so much legalistically asserted as it is effectively demonstrated. The authority which was given to the disciples, for example, was manifested in the power of their message and ministry to release man from the bondage of sin and to give him the power to lead the Christian life in trust and in love. This power, of course, is ultimately ascribed to God alone. Again and again in the Acts of the Apostles it is insisted that because the Holy Spirit was at work through the life and fellowship and mission of the apostolic church it had, therefore, an authority and power to accomplish God's work and purpose among men. The apostolic church had authority, "being full of the Holy Ghost."

The concern of the early church in developing authoritative forms and orders within its life was precisely that the liberating message of the gospel and all its power and effectiveness might everywhere be heard and believed and practiced. The development of the monarchial episcopacy (that is, the authoritative rule of one bishop in each large community), of the canon of scripture, of the creeds and other formulations of the ecumenical councils—all these were designed to safeguard the original integrity and power of the Christian message rather than to establish some legalistic and authoritarian structure to which individual Christians were to be blindly and unquestioningly subservient. The more one reads the history of the first four centuries of the church the more one is impressed with the caution and reserve with which authoritarian structures were developed. The great decisions of the ecumenical councils, for example, did, of course, rule out certain misunderstandings of the Christian message, but equally impressive is the fact that they are allowed large room for varieties of understanding and interpretation. The descriptions that we have of church life of the time suggest no oppressive and tyrannous despotism on the part of the bishops but, for the most part (though one must confess that there are distressing exceptions), a willingness to leave much freedom and much independence to individual clergy and congregations and even to individual believers.

It is not possible here to discuss the ways in which this original Christian conception of authority became in other periods and circumstances corrupted by serious abuse. It is sufficient to say that the Anglican Reformation sought to recover this ancient conception of authority as designed primarily to secure the achievement of freedom and liberty for Christians. It is perhaps difficult to commend this Anglican settlement to American readers who are familiar with the principle of separation of church and state. It must be granted that the Elizabethan religious settlement knew no such principle and that it employed the power of the state to secure religious conformity. We should not let our disappointment with this failure of the fathers of the English Reformation to appreciate fully the principle of religious toleration lead us to overlook the significance of the forward step in the achievement of a balance between authority and liberty which the English Reformation does demonstrate. The participation of the Crown and of Parliament in the religious decisions of the English nation is of the greatest significance. Not only the bishops and higher clergy were asked to determine the form of the prayer book, the number of dioceses, and other important ecclesiastical questions, but these were matters for prolonged parliamentary debate and for consideration by the Crown and its counselors.

At the same time, it was recognized that the great central matters of the Christian faith were not, of course, subject to revision or amendment. Anglican respect for tradition precluded any radical innovations in matters which Christians had always regarded as crucial, necessary, and central. The role of the bishops and other clergy in preaching and administering the sacraments was generally recognized and safeguarded. It is true that hot-headed Tudor and Stuart monarchs and equally hot-headed Parliaments sometimes overstepped the boundaries in such matters which the general consensus of the English Church had established. Archbishop Laud refers in some of his writings to the unfortunate example of the Emperor Constantius who, as he says, "meddled in determining, and that beforehand, what the prelates should do . . . but then we must know withal, that Athanasius reckoned him for this, as that antichrist which Daniel prophesied of!" The teaching function of the clergy and more especially of the episcopate held its ground even against the proud blusterings of Parliament or the monarchy. There are limits to democracy in any church which can claim the name of Christian. The authentic Christian gospel is not established by a majority vote; it comes down from two thousand years of Christian experience and testimony which has overwhelming weight and authority. What is significant, however, is that this weight and authority are freely acknowledged and accepted by representative assemblies drawn from both the clerical and lay orders of the church. This important idea was insisted upon in the

Anglican Reformation and formed a basis for the even more thoroughgoing democratization of the church which took place in America.

It has often been observed that the fathers of the American Constitution were also the fathers of the Constitution and Canons of the Episcopal Church in America. Their wisdom is equally evident in both documents. On the one hand, laymen are invited to share in all the deliberative, judicial, and administrative functions of the church. When first introduced, these proposals brought forth a storm of disapproval. Most offensive to the traditionalist was the suggestion that laymen could sit on trial courts for the discipline and possible deposition of presbyters and bishops. One shocked comment of the period, reflecting social snobbery perhaps as much as ecclesiastical conservatism, speculated that the bishop's barber might shave him in the morning "and in the afternoon vote him out of office." Despite such opposition, however, the right of the layman to participate at all levels of the church's legislative, executive, and judicial life was strongly affirmed. Great authority and responsibility were vested in the parish congregation, which in turn elected a vestry and delegates to a diocesan convention. So strong was the democratic tide in the early days of America that in many Atlantic seaboard dioceses the bishop was not even allowed to enter a church to perform ecclesiastical or sacramental acts without the invitation and consent of the vestry or the rector! The laity of the church may exercise a decisive veto both in the diocesan and general conventions of the church. A "vote by orders" means that both the clergy and the laity, voting separately, must give a concurrent majority if a measure is to pass.

The principle of "checks and balances" also operates in the functioning of the episcopacy. A careful reading of the Constitution and Canons of the Episcopal Church and of most of its constituent dioceses will reveal that the bishop is able to do very few things on his own sole authority. Again and again he is obliged to secure the consent of this or that committee or group of advisers before his action can be taken as authoritative. No man can be ordained, for example, without a long series of approvals and recommendations in which the laity of the church by their designated representatives must participate. Although the bishop is given the authority of extending the work of the church within the boundaries of his own diocese, the clergy and laity control the budgetary and financial support of such work, and therefore participate in the development of policy and program. The laity of the Episcopal Church may exercise the power of veto in all changes in the liturgy, in the election of bishops, and on many other centrally important matters in church life. Obviously the Episcopal Church, reflecting the spirit and ideals of the American Constitution, intends to be thoroughly democratic and representative in its life and government.

This important role of the laity in the life and government of the church involves, of course, important responsibilities for each layman. He is always, except in the most unusual circumstances, a member of some particular congregation. When he is confirmed he is enrolled in the list of his congregation and as soon as he is an adult has the right and responsibility of taking part in the major decisions which the congregation makes, especially through the election of members of the vestry. The parish is incorporated under the laws of the state in which it exists, and to the whole assembly of members of the parish is given the ultimate responsibility of determining the constitution and by-laws of the parish corporation under which the vestry functions. To the vestry is given, in most dioceses of the country, very large authority in the calling of a rector. In some dioceses the bishop participates in the selection, and in all dioceses he must give his consent before any final choice is made.

The vestry or parish meeting also elects deputies to a diocesan convention, which, as we have said, is the supreme legislative authority in a diocese. There are 98 dioceses in the Episcopal Church. The diocesan convention has the sole authority and responsibility for electing its bishop. In a large diocese suffragan—assistant—bishops are sometimes needed, and the diocesan convention has the responsibility of providing such assistance if the bishop of the diocese requests it and the convention believes his request is justified. Again, however, the principle of "checks and balances" operates, and no diocese is allowed to elect bishops without the approval of other bishops and other dioceses. This insures that only broadly representative men and women who command the respect of the whole church can be elevated to these important positions of leadership.

Each diocese elects deputies to the supreme legislative authority of the Episcopal Church, namely, the General Convention. Here, following the manner of the United States Constitution, two legislative houses are provided for and must concur in any legislation. As has also been pointed out already, the laity and the clergy who make up the House of Deputies may with proper parliamentary procedure require separate voting so that both laity and clergy must concur. In the General Convention is vested the ultimate responsibility for the development of the Constitution and Canon Law of the church and the promotion and development of its overall missionary program. The House of Bishops, although it can pass no legislation without the concurrence of the House of Deputies, has for many years made it a practice from time to time to issue pastoral letters, dealing with important aspects of church life or with moral or ethical issues in the life of the church, the nation, and the world. Such pastoral letters must be read or otherwise made available in every congregation of the church.

The supreme executive official of the Episcopal

Church is the Presiding Bishop, chosen by a majority vote of the House of Bishops and confirmed by the majority vote of the House of Deputies. Upon election to this office, he resigns from whatever diocesan position he has held and remains as Presiding Bishop for nine years. His main responsibilities are the direction of the missionary, educational, promotional, and social relations aspects of the church's program, and the presidency of the House of Bishops, in which function he also supervises the arrangements for the certification of election and the consecration of new bishops. Like the presidency of the United States, the office of Presiding Bishop depends for its power and effectiveness to a very great extent upon the character and leadership of the person in office. However, in recent years canonical legislation has tended to increase the responsibilities and authority of the Presiding Bishop, so that he is now a much more important person in the eyes of the church than he was a century ago.

In this thoroughly democratic organization, however, the traditional spiritual prerogatives of the bishops and the clergy are carefully maintained. Although a clergyman cannot be forced upon a congregation against its will, neither can the congregation dissolve the pastoral relationship between itself and its rector without due process, including the bishop's consent and concurrence. As a result, there is a respect for the independence and integrity of the rector in the exercise of his spiritual duties. There are few other democratically organized churches in which the freedom of the minister in the pulpit is so carefully safeguarded. This is not to say that a priest does not have difficulties when he espouses unpopular causes, but he has behind him a certain weight of tradition as well as the provisions of canon law which defend and sustain his rights.

This is not only true with respect to preaching, but in the very important question of the admission and excommunication of members. It is the rector's responsibility to see to it that candidates for baptism and confirmation are properly instructed in the elements of the Christian faith and in their responsibilities as Christians. No Episcopal rector would have the problem which arose years ago for a friend of mine, a minister of a highly democratically organized congregation of another protestant communion, whose efforts to integrate black church members into his congregation were vetoed by an adverse vote of the congregation. In that very same community, I was able to present black candidates for baptism and confirmation, to welcome them at the communion rail, and to integrate them into the spiritual life of the parish without any questions being raised about my right to do so. This was done in spite of the fact that I knew that at least a small number of the members of my congregation disapproved of development of a racially integrated parish. Episcopal clergy, of course, will in the exercise of their responsibilities want to be "as wise as serpents and harmless as doves" and will usually try not to get too far ahead of their congregations in the exercise of their spiritual privileges. This is a part of any priest's pastoral responsibility. This freedom, however, does enable him to embody the prophetic tradition of the Christian ministry even against rather overwhelming opposition in his congregation in a way that is scarcely possible when the ministerial tenure may be revoked by a simple majority of a congregational meeting.

Likewise, to the minister, acting under the supervision of the bishop, is given the awesome responsibility of excommunication. By the rubrics of the prayer book a priest is directed to speak to anyone living a "notoriously evil life" and to tell the person not to come to the Holy Table until there is clear proof of repentance and amendment of life. The same procedure is to be followed "with those who have done wrong to their neighbors and are a scandal to the other members of the congregation," disallowing communion until there is evidence of restitution. Further, when the priest sees there is hatred between members, he must speak privately with them and tell them they may not receive communion until they are prepared to forgive each other. Flouting the Christian ethic of love and its standards calls into question the whole character and ideal of Christian discipleship and must be dealt with. The priest must give notice to the bishop of any such acts of excommunication, with the implied suggestion that the bishop will consult and advise with him about his decisions. Here again it would seem to be a wise provision which vests responsibility for the most serious acts of ecclesiastical discipline, namely, excommunication, in the hands of one who by reason of his pastoral responsibilities and wisdom will have better knowledge of background and motives than will the members of a congregation.

In a very similar manner, despite all the checks and balances the operation of which has been described here as limiting and defining the role of the bishop in the church, there is a genuine and deeply felt respect for the spiritual responsibilities which the office has traditionally embodied in the Christian church. The bishop may have very little legal or constitutional power but the office's prestige and moral authority are, however, incalculable and widely felt. The prophetic role of some of the bishops of the American church testifies to the possibilities of the episcopal office, fulfilling in modern times some of the best elements in the tradition which stretches from Ambrose to Thomas à Becket to William Temple.

This respect for the episcopal office does not depend upon any particular theory about the origin of the episcopal office in the church. Not all Episcopalians agree in their theories about how the office of a bishop came to hold the place it has held in most branches of the Christian church since the middle of the second century. All Episcopalians would agree, probably, in affirming the idea of Apostolic Succession in the sense that the bishop exercises in the contemporary church the same role which the Apostles exercised in the church during the years immediately following the Resurrection. Episcopalians differ, however, as to whether this continuation of influence and responsibility was the result of a direct command of our Lord or whether it developed in the life of the early church under the guidance of the Holy Spirit. The resolution of this question has seemed to many Episcopalians—of which I would count myself one—to be in large part a question of historical evidence. Since the historical evidence in question is in some ways inconclusive, it has never seemed to me to be possible to make a necessary dogma out of what can only be a tentative historical hypothesis. It is interesting that in the early debates of Elizabethan Anglicans with Puritan opponents over the question of the place of the bishop in the church, it was the Puritans and not the Anglicans who sought to fix the answer to the question by means of resort to biblical texts. Many Anglican apologists were willing to say that the role of the bishop in the church was developed not as a result of our Lord's command but as a convenient and reasonable arrangement of church life which could be justified by its ability to secure the unity and continuity of the church.

To an Anglican, centuries of tradition carry their own persuasiveness. The values and importance of the Episcopal office can, however, be demonstrated in terms of present-day effectiveness. There are, for example, obvious advantages to investing authority and symbolizing continuity in a single person. The success of the Episcopal Church in America, for example, in avoiding endless divisions and schisms over relatively obscure points of theology or because of geographical and cultural differences is impressive, especially by contrast with the proliferation of groups holding to a congregational or presbyterian type of polity. One of the most notable instances of this success was the reunion of the Northern and Southern Episcopal dioceses immediately after the close of the Civil War. Although, of course, the Southern states organized an Episcopal Church in the Confederacy, it completely disappeared and Southern church members found their way back into union with the Northern church within a few years of Appomattox. The one sizable group of Episcopalians, the so-called Reformed Episcopal Church, to separate itself from the main body of the Episcopal Church in the history of America, has had such a limited growth that most Episcopalians are not even aware it exists. Part of the reason for this remarkable maintenance of unity and solidarity in a vast and sprawling nation with strong inclinations toward independence of action and thinking is due almost entirely to the importance that is ascribed to the office of the bishop. The ancient injunction of St. Ignatius, "do nothing without the bishop," has maintained the unified and catholic conception of the church in the midst of many tensions and differences both theological and cultural.

Surely one of the most important reasons why I am an Episcopalian is that I have found here a church which seems to me to make great room for the truths of democracy and of congregational initiative and responsibility, and has at the same time defended the spiritual integrity of the ministry and maintained the spiritual unity of the church through the retention of the age-old conceptions of ministerial and, more especially, episcopal authority.

Seven

In The World

In the midst of the turbulent social crises which shook and challenged the United States during my college years, it was inevitable that my relationship to the Episcopal Church should be judged in part upon the quality of social thinking and social action which that church seemed to me to demonstrate. To the outsider the Episcopal Church has often been represented as being composed almost exclusively of the very wealthy, aristocratic and, as a result, highly conservative members of society. It may be true that in some places it does bear that aspect, although my own experience has been that this characterization of the Episcopal Church is almost everywhere a caricature of the facts. I admit that I was somewhat shaken during the 1930's to read indictments of the Episcopal Church by men like Upton Sinclair, and I remember sharing his sense of shock at the fact that the wife of one of the prominent bishops of the church in the 1900's had reported to the police a loss of more than

$25,000 in jewelry! Mr. Sinclair's scorching contrast between this state of affairs and the simplicity of the Carpenter of Nazareth was probably more persuasive than logical, but it made a deep impression upon me.

The fact is that the Episcopal Church's concern with social problems and its ability to stimulate in a surprisingly large number of members a fairly liberal point of view about social and political affairs is at least as important a part of its tradition as its reputation for attracting the privileged and well-born. The Church of England, for example, from which the Episcopal Church stems, has always conceived itself as responsible for the moral and spiritual welfare of the whole body of English society. A history of constructive proposals for social reform can be traced from the sermons of Hugh Latimer, one of the Reformation bishops, martyred under Queen Mary, through Archbishop Laud, to William Wilberforce and the "Clapham Sect," to the activities of the members of the 19th-century Broad Church like Charles Kingsley and Frederick Denison Maurice and such Anglo-Catholic social thinkers as Charles Gore or V.A. Demant. A church which could produce, for example, a Charles Kingsley who, on April 10, 1848, addressed a challenging message to the great Chartist gathering then being held in London, a message which was entitled "Working Men of England!" and was signed "A Working Parson," is obviously not a church accurately to be described as "the Tory Party at prayer."

From the point of view of our American prejudice in favor of a separation of church and state, it may be difficult to appreciate the advantages in social outlook which can conceivably result from an established ecclesiastical body. Whatever disadvantages establishment may have, it does not necessarily result in a subservient or complacent Christian church; at least it has not done so in the case of the Church of England. What it does produce is a sense of identification with the problems and issues which confront the national society, with a full acceptance of all the responsibilities that involvement in such questions carries with it. The sectarian ideal of the relationship of Christianity to society—an ideal which has been very influential in shaping protestant social thought in America, for example—tends to think of the church as an other-worldly society, sharply separated in its habits and thinking from the national society around it. Its primary obligation is to save people out of the national society rather than to save them *within* it. Its social message is often cast in a form of a scolding rebuke directed toward rather clearly defined "worldly" practices. The Church of England, of course, knew something of this spirit in the Evangelical Movement, especially as it arose under the influence of John Wesley and his colleagues in the late 18th century. By and large, however, Anglicanism has taken a much broader view of its social responsibilities than that and has been willing to accept the legitimacy of the world and its ways, seeking only within them to achieve higher levels of justice, freedom and mutuality.

A church which seems by its moral teaching and social message to equate drinking a martini with suppressing the right of workmen to organize a labor union, would appear to be in danger of confusing "tithing mint, anise, and cummin" with "the weightier matters of the law." It has been painful to one who believes in the possibilities of united protestant witness to observe how many times the only social program about which many protestant ministers and church leaders get really excited is the banning of beer advertising on billboards, when a whole host of injustices and social evils in the community clamor for rebuke and reform. The Episcopal Church is often regarded as being hopelessly worldly in its outlook. No Episcopalian can afford to dismiss this charge without seriously thinking about it, but to equate worldliness with an acceptance of harmless social habits and the identification of social wickedness with such habits will always seem to an Episcopalian to involve the equal danger of moralism, censoriousness, and an asceticism that comes perilously close to denying the goodness of God's creation.

In the tumultuous social and political controversies of the 1930's I was looking for a church which took social problems with utter seriousness. In many ways the Episcopal Church filled the bill. Like many other young people of the time, I was deeply impressed with the economic and ethical persuasiveness of socialism. Somewhat to my surprise, I found a respectable tradition of long standing within Anglicanism which was willing to call itself "Christian Socialism." The movement in the Church of England which bore this name derived chiefly from the labors of the famous Frederick Denison Maurice, but it was carried on and had a more sustained impact upon church thinking through the work of several Anglo-Catholics, principally Bishop Charles Gore and Canon Henry Scott Holland. Their general conviction was summed up in these words of Gore: "They were all at once in feeling that the principles and life and spirit of Jesus Christ had very much to do with the social question, and would be found on serious investigation to have both an illuminating power to be brought to bear on the relation of man to man and a force in the struggle against injustice and the exploiting of the weak, which could not be equaled anywhere else."*

This point of view had great influence and was given frequent expression in the Episcopal Church, especially between 1910 and 1940. Bishops' pastoral letters and the minutes of many diocesan and General Conventions during that period reflect the church's intention to speak critically and constructively about the conditions of social life. During my college and seminary days the Church League for Industrial Democracy was actively at work,

---

*Quoted in Fletcher, Jos. F., and Miller, Spencer, *The Church and Industry* (Longmans, Green & Co, 1930), page 20.

influencing large numbers of younger clergy especially and occupying an important, even if unofficial, part in the program of every General Convention. In 1940, for example, Bishop Edward L. Parsons of California explained the attitude of the CLID, as it was known, to a reporter in the following words: "What is wrong is the social order which expresses . . . the selfishness and blindness of the human heart; a social order which makes most Christians deny daily the essential meaning of their faith; a social order which puts the emphasis upon wealth and power, and consecrates the sin of avarice."*

In more recent years the response of the Episcopal Church to social issues and concerns has not been focused in any special organization so much as in generalized and official action on the part of the church as a whole. The issue of black empowerment, raised by Presiding Bishop John E. Hines at the General Convention of 1967 has already been referred to, but efforts have also been made to share and respond to the aspirations of other ethnic and racial groups as well as young people and women. The inclusion of representative members of such people in the church's legislative and policy-making bodies has had much to do with keeping the Episcopal Church alert and responsive to movements for justice and human dignity in the society and the nation and the world. The role of the Episcopal Church in these areas

---

Kansas City Times, Thursday, October 10, 1940, page 5.

has been a pioneering and dramatic one in the past several decades.

The early Anglo-Catholic Christian Socialists insisted that in the sacramental character of the Christian church lay one of the most dynamic motivations for greater fellowship among people of all classes and races and nations. To the extent that the Episcopal Church is a sacramental church, stressing equally the importance of the new relationship to God which is made possible in Christ and the new relationship which is similarly made possible between a man and his brother, it has always seemed to me to have a special opportunity to demonstrate the social imperative of the Christian faith. I well remember how in my days of enthusiasm for the New Deal I was impressed by the ways in which Episcopalians like Frances Perkins and Henry Wallace so obviously drew the inspiration for their political and social attitudes and policies from their sacramental life.

It would be very misleading to suggest, however, that all Episcopalians will read these last few paragraphs with unmixed enthusiasm. The Episcopal Church has at least its quota of social conservatives and even of social reactionaries. As I have grown older I have become somewhat more realistic about the possibilities of using the church as a kind of advance guard in social and political thinking. Too often the stirring resolutions which used to warm my heart in my student days were not really representative of the thinking of the average church member. I have become somewhat more suspicious of the maneuvers of well-meaning clergy and sometimes laity who seek to carry on social and political matters which represent in reality the convictions of only a fraction of those in attendance. For all that I have said about the tradition of social leadership which exists in the Anglican Communion and in the Episcopal Church, I still suspect that my own political thinking would be far to the left of that which would be revealed in a real Gallop poll of Episcopalian opinion! Sometimes the contrast is painful and shocking, and if I had retained only my naive faith as a college senior that the Episcopal Church was chiefly important as a rallying point for advanced social and political thinking, I should have abandoned that church some time ago. Like many other Americans of my generation, however, I have come to have a new respect for the contributions of the genuine conservative, and I rejoice that both conservative and liberal versions of a Christian's political and social responsibility can exist together in the Episcopal Church with opportunities of confronting each other in study and thought, in worship and discussion. Once again the tradition of pulpit freedom, for example, has new significance for me and seems more than ever to be one of the strong points of the Episcopal Church. My own inclination would be to put more hope in the development of voluntary groups organized perhaps along vocational or special interest lines. The Episcopal Peace Fellowship and the

Union of Black Episcopalians are examples of the kind of frontline thinking and prodding which is needed to keep the church abreast of the needs of the whole society. Perhaps a widespread recovery of concern for social transformation will have to take place within our society before this aspect of the church's life will come once more into its own. I am content that an impressive tradition exists within Anglicanism and lives on today in the prophetic speaking and thinking of many of our bishops, clergy, and leading lay persons.

The social responsibility of a Christian is not exhausted, of course, in projects and hopes for the reformation of social institutions and political organizations. Like many other Christian bodies, the Episcopal Church has also taken a leading role in many American communities in sponsoring and encouraging a whole host of agencies which seek to minister to men and women and children in special cases of emergency and need. Hospitals, institutions for child care, homes for aged people, services to underprivileged people and neighborhoods through programs of recreation and fellowship, a ministry to indigent people needing counsel and financial help and to inmates of public institutions of care and correction—in all of these ways the Episcopal Church has established a notable record for good works and for neighborly service that is a source of pride and humble gratitude to any one of her members. More than most other protestant groups the Episcopal

Church has given special attention to ministry in public institutions, especially jails, penitentiaries, mental institutions, poor farms, reformatories, and other ministries. This specialization reflects the genius for pastoral care which I think is one of the distinctive marks of Anglicanism. Perhaps again because of its sacramental character, the Episcopal Church seems to rely less than other protestant bodies on sermons and exhortations. The impersonality and democracy of a service like the Holy Communion makes it eloquent of divine forgiveness and human acceptance when it is celebrated in a penitentiary or an institution for psychiatric care. Someone once pointed out that there were more Episcopalians than any other non-Roman Catholic group of Christians in San Quentin Penitentiary! I prefer to believe that this is evidence of the pastoral outreach of the Episcopal Church in such an institution rather than an indication of an inherent tendency to delinquency in people who worship by a prayer book!

The America of my college days has greatly changed and my earlier criteria of what constituted a prophetic and socially concerned church have changed too. Nevertheless, I still believe that few other religious bodies can match the wisdom and the breadth and the understanding with which the Episcopal Church conceives and tackles its task of serving the human family and lifting it to higher levels of justice and mutuality. This is one of the reasons I am an Episcopalian.

Eight

Oneness In Christ

Although I became an Episcopalian after having spent the major part of my childhood in contact with other church traditions, I believe I have somehow avoided the temptation which besets so many converts, namely, to minimize the importance and validity of other Christian bodies. Especially in the American scene, where the Episcopal Church is often a very small minority of the total religiously committed population, it is pompous and foolish—as well as profoundly unchristian—to assume that the only authentic Christian experience is to be found in the Episcopal Church and that the endless praises of heaven are probably being conducted according to the prayer book of 1549! This is only a slightly caricatured version of an unconscious assumption by a good many Episcopalians and may derive in part from the fact that the Episcopal Church is made up so largely of people who have come into it from other religious traditions. I cannot imagine quite how I escaped falling into something of this attitude myself, since I find that I am often tempted beyond my strength to be dogmatic and to absolutize my preferences and tastes.

Part of the credit ought to be given to a unique inter-faith organization in southern California to which I was introduced in my college years. It was the University Religious Conference, a cooperative undertaking supported by the outstanding religious leadership of the southern California community, including the Roman Catholic Archbishop, the Episcopal Bishop, one of the leading Jewish rabbis, and almost every important religious official in the area. Because of its representative character, the University Religious Conference was never tempted to suggest that important differences of creedal viewpoint could be waived aside as insignificant. Its motto was: "We agree to disagree agreeably." In the building provided by this unique and exciting organization, the religious activities at the University of California at Los Angeles, barred by state law from using the campus facilities themselves, took place. In my senior year in college I lived and worked in this building, and on the basis of my services as dishwasher, waiter, and occasionally assistant to the cook, I can claim a first-hand knowledge of interfaith affairs, especially as seen from the perspective of dietary peculiarities!

In such a setting, it was inevitable that personal friendships would spring up across religious lines, and that occasional instances of official cooperation would take place. In later years I often spoke as the representative of the protestant tradition along with Roman Catholic and Jewish friends on the familiar "trialogue" pattern, a responsibility which helped to focus areas both of agreement and disagreement among the major religious traditions as well as within the protestant family of communions and denominations. Two years at the Yale Divinity School, an interdenominational graduate school of theology, helped to broaden my knowledge and interest in other religious groups as well as to reinforce my own convictions and preferences with respect to Anglicanism. Like many other working clergy, I have participated always in ministerial associations and church federations, a responsibility which I have always thought a minister owes some time to, even if the experience is not always very rewarding. All of this background was useful as I sought for thirteen years to administer the religious program of Columbia University, where every conceivable religious position, not only of the American variety but from all over the world, was represented.

The Episcopal Church has an important role to play, in the first place, in the development of the characteristically American interfaith movement. I know of no other single church which is able to understand so fully the distinctive outlooks both of protestantism and of Roman Catholicism as is the Episcopal Church. What is more, its deep reliance upon the Bible, its wide use of the Psalms in its worship, and its specification for both Old Testament and New Testament lessons in its Daily Offices, gives it a natural affinity with and understanding of Judaism. Elizabethan Anglicanism has bequeathed a curious kind of ironic inclusiveness to its daughter churches. This does not mean, of course, that theological orthodoxy is taken lightly. We shall see presently that the very opposite is the case. There is, however, an almost indefinable sense of the proprieties of interfaith contact which has its roots, I believe, in the relationships to Roman Catholicism and Judaism which have just been referred to. If the interfaith movement in America is to achieve its maximum potentialities, it must continue to move from the realm of mere polite gestures to genuine theological discussion and encounter. I believe that the Anglican tradition has a very special contribution to make to this kind of undertaking.

I have been increasingly aware that the Episcopal Church has what seems to me an enormous advantage in interdenominational activities within non-Roman Christianity. In the first place, the problem of the character and life of the church is considered in Anglicanism to be a matter of the deepest importance. In contrast to certain other protestant churches of a more sectarian tradition, Anglicanism has always insisted that the life of the church and her sacraments must be thought of as necessary "means of grace." Church life is not an elective which a Christian may take on out of a sense of duty and responsibility but may omit without serious damage to his faith. The fact is he cannot really be a Christian apart from involvement in the community of believers.

Anglicanism, furthermore, has always had a lively interest in the unity of the church. Of course, no Christian who takes the Bible seriously can overlook the importance of maintaining a visible witness in a united Christian fellowship to the reconciling power of the love of God in Christ. "That they may be one" was not only a pious aspiration of our Lord's but was his description of one of the church's essential characteristics. One of the advantages of the background of an established church is that it gives seriousness and urgency to the problem of expressing in one broad ecclesiastical framework as inclusive a sampling of the varieties of Christian attitude and discipleship as possible. From the very beginnings of the Reformation, Anglican leaders exhibited the greatest concern for the cause of Christian unity. Church historians tell us that Archbishop Cranmer, for example, urged in vain that some of the continental leaders, chiefly Melancthon, draw together a representative group of continental protestant leaders for conference and consultation with the Anglicans in order to secure a unification of the Reformation forces. Richard Hooker, in his *Laws of Ecclesiastical Polity*, urges that differences of theological emphasis, for example, ought not to be encouraged among the several national churches that shared in the Reformation movement, but ought to be reserved for resolution at a broadly representative conference that he hopes will be called before too long. The Reformation churches, according to Hooker, would have been wise to have adopted their distinctive positions and established their ministry and polity "in more wary and suspense manner, as being to stand in force until God should give the opportunity of some general conference what might be best for every of them afterward to do" (*Laws of Ecclesiastical Polity*, Preface, II, 2).

It was, therefore, perhaps with some inevitability that the Episcopal Church took a leading role in the initiation of what has now come to be called the Ecumenical Movement. Indeed, no other religious body except the Disciples of Christ can claim to have done more. Beginning in the middle of the 19th century the Episcopal Church, which by that time was clearly destined to be outnumbered in the United States by other church bodies which had pressed into the frontier areas of the west more rapidly, began to consider seriously what we would now call ecumenical questions. William Augustus Muhlenberg, rector of the Church of the Holy Communion in New York City, focused this interest by his famous "Memorial" addressed to the House of Bishops in 1853. In it he proposed that ministers of other Christian bodies be given episcopal ordination without, however, abandoning their original denominational affiliation. As a condition for such an ordination they were to be committed to the use of certain portions of the Book of Common Prayer but were not expected to conform in other ways to the doctrine, discipline, or worship of the Episcopal Church. The "Memorial" got a fairly chilly response, but it had the merit of raising an important question, consideration of which was postponed, however, by the urgencies of the Civil War.

The question of the role of the Episcopal Church in ecumenical activity was raised again in the 1870's by William Reed Huntington, the influential rector of Grace Church in New York City, who proposed the setting forth of four points on the basis of which the Episcopal Church would be prepared to discuss organic union with other Christian bodies. These four points—the recognition of Holy Scripture as the supreme theological authority in the church, the acceptance and use of the two historic creeds (Apostles' and Nicene) as a sufficient summary of the faith of the church, the unfailing use of the two sacraments instituted by Christ (Baptism and Holy Communion), and the historic episcopate, adopted to local conditions, as the basis of the church's ministry and polity—were accepted by the House of Bishops in 1886 and in 1888 were approved by the Lambeth Conference of Anglican bishops as outlining Anglicanism's platform for Christian reunion. The General Convention at Louisville in 1973 reaffirmed what is known as the Chicago-Lambeth Quadrilateral.

Another kind of ecumenical activity which has had wide-reaching importance was initiated by the

Episcopal Church. Charles Henry Brent, Bishop of the Philippine Islands and later of Western New York, introduced at the General Convention of 1910 at Cincinnati the proposal which led to the great World Conferences on Faith and Order and later on Life and Work and which brought about the establishment of the World Council of Churches. Characteristically, Bishop Brent's proposal did not suggest cavalier dismissal of theological and ecclesiastical differences but proposed only that by means of conference and consultation the real nature of these differences might be investigated and the areas of agreement and disagreement clearly delineated.

This does not mean that the Episcopal Church cannot find ways, consistent with her commitment to Episcopal polity, to participate in experiments in merged congregations with churches that do not accept the importance and desirability of Episcopal ordination. Several such experiments, some of fairly long-standing, flourish in some of our dioceses, including the diocese where I served as bishop. But such experiments must provide for a sacramental ministry by an episcopally ordained priest if it is to be loyal to the Anglican tradition.

The participation of the Episcopal Church in the Consultation on Church Union, consisting of several denominational church bodies, has provided an opportunity to defend and explain the significance which the episcopate has for the Anglican experience. This issue has proved to be a difficult one in the

Consultation, and a Plan of Union drawn up in 1972 foundered upon the rock of strong differences in viewpoint on precisely this point. At the same time the Episcopal Church has shown flexibility in adapting her commitment to episcopal ordination within ecumenical experiments. In the Houston General Convention of 1970, for example, authority was given to use the liturgy for the celebration of Holy Communion developed by the Consultation on Church Union, and Episcopalians were encouraged to participate in ecumenical services using that liturgy, providing an episcopally ordained priest was the celebrant, or one of a number of concelebrants. Although this resolution was not re-affirmed at the Louisville Convention of 1973, it is difficult not to assume that this represented a permanent break-through in ecumenical relations on the sticky issue of episcopal ordination.

One of the most promising areas of ecumenical discussion which the Episcopal Church—and indeed the whole Anglican Communion—was involved in during the past few decades was with the Roman Catholics. To the surprise of many observers agreement was reached by representative commissions of theologians on the doctrines of these two great traditions. In several areas of the United States covenant agreements brought together Episcopal and Roman Catholic parishes. The agreements usually provided for mutual prayers for one another's congregations, pulpit exchanges, cooperation in many areas of community service and Christian witness, and other manifestations of Christian unity. There was genuine hope that the day of mutual recognition of ministries and of full intercommunion between the Anglican and Roman Catholic churches might not be far off, but progress has stalled, most evidently on the issue of ordination of women to priesthood and the episcopate.

At present the most promising ecumenical discussions involve Anglicans and Lutherans in Europe and America, and at this writing the Episcopal Church and the Lutheran Church in America are seriously considering intercommunion, a move which would signal a dramatic step forward in the Ecumenical Movement worldwide.

Not all that calls itself ecumenical has necessarily any affinity to the world movement that usually goes by this name. Much cooperative American protestant activity, especially on the local level, is on a very shallow and superficial basis. I have been as active as anyone else in the field of cooperative protestantism, and have served as president of a great metropolitan church federation and in another instance led in the formation of a community council of churches. I must confess that I have often been in despair, however, at the unwillingness of many American protestants to discuss the significant theological differences which separate them or to come to any kind of profound agreement about the meaning of the Christian faith and its relationship to community life. It is often simply assumed that such agreement exists, but at any moment a critical issue may arise which makes it perfectly evident how unwarranted this assumption is. One of the reasons I am an Episcopalian is because I believe the Episcopal Church with its broad theological platform, consisting of the great essentials of the Christian faith, and its witness by its apostolic ministry to the continuity of the Christian tradition down through the centuries, has an important contribution to make to ecumenical Christianity. The leadership given to the Ecumenical Movement by such undeniably orthodox Anglican leaders as Bishop Charles Brent or Archbishop William Temple disproves the allegation that such participation involves any lessening of loyalty to Anglicanism itself. The breadth of such a document, for example, as the "Letter to All Christian People" from the Lambeth Conference of 1920 ought to reassure but also to challenge the cautious and conservative among us: "We believe that God wills fellowship . . .; we believe that it is God's purpose to manifest this fellowship . . . in an outward, visible and united society, holding one faith, having its own recognized officers, using God's given means of grace, and inspiring all its members to the worldwide service of the Kingdom of God. This is what we mean by the Catholic Church . . . this united fellowship is not visible in the world today. . . . The vision which rises before us is that of a Church genuinely Catholic, loyal to all Truth, and gathering into its fellowship all who profess and call themselves Christians. . . . May we not reasonably claim that the Episcopate is one means of providing . . . a ministry acknowledged by every part of the Church? . . . It is not that we call in question for a moment the spiritual reality of the ministries of those Communions who do not possess the Episcopate. On the contrary, we thankfully acknowledge that these ministries have been manifestly blessed and owned by the Holy Spirit as effective means of grace."

To any Christian who is drawn to the Episcopal Church but feels that its slow and cautious approach to the question of Christian reunion may be hindering the advancement of that important purpose, there is reassurance to be found in the Church of South India. The lesson of the Church of South India and of similarly unified church bodies in Southeast Asia is instructive. The distinctive things for which Anglicanism stands—the spiritual authority of the bishop as the shepherd and teacher of the flock of Christ, and an indigenous liturgy based upon the proportion of faith as it is demonstrated in the historic creeds and the traditional sacraments of Baptism and the Holy Communion—have been enthusiastically received and claimed by the non-Anglicans who have entered into the United Churches. It is possible that many non-Episcopalians are held back from a recognition of the validity of the episcopal form of government and the advantages of a liturgy primarily by the exclusive claims and the air of superiority with which these treasures are treated by Anglicans themselves! Because it seems to me that the Anglican Communion has discovered an important secret of Christian unity and an important clue to the path along which Christian reunion will be achieved, I rejoice in my membership in that communion and only pray that it may more and more make its full contribution to the achievement of the purpose of the great Shepherd and Bishop of our souls "that they all may be one."

Nine

Mission

To be an Episcopalian, of course, involves one at once in membership in an extraordinarily close-knit, worldwide fellowship known as the Anglican Communion. It used to be said that "the sun never sets on the British Empire" and for this reason it is still true today that the sun never sets on the Anglican Communion, which has sprung up wherever English-speaking people have gone. In every continent of the world, drawn from every major racial group, Anglicanism represents an important and distinctive tradition within the great worldwide Christian Church. It embraces more than 500 dioceses and includes over 70 million baptized members.

The vast and variegated company of Christians is held together not by any legal structure nor official ecclesiastical connections but by its loyalty to the essential ideals of the English Reformation, namely, episcopal government by apostolic succession, liturgical worship, the Bible interpreted by the creeds and tradition as the source of doctrine. Since the oldest see in the Anglican Communion is that of Canterbury, the Archbishop is regarded as *primus inter pares* (first among equals) in respect and veneration. The late Archbishop Michael Ramsey and his successors, by their world travels, have contributed impressively to the growing sense of Anglican unity around the world and have helped to symbolize and express the Anglican ideal of reformed catholic Christianity. In the latter part of the 19th century meetings of all the Anglican bishops began to take place at regular intervals. Since these meetings took place under the presidency of the Archbishop of Canterbury at his palace they were called "Lambeth Conferences." Beginning in 1960 this worldwide Anglican fellowship took on some structure and a modest amount of executive and legislative machinery.

The Anglican Consultative Council was formed and symbolizes and promotes the common mission of the churches in communion with the See of Canterbury. The ACC's Secretary General's office is in London, but ACC meetings are held in various parts of the world.

From the day of Pentecost, it has been one of the glories of the Christian church that it is able to transcend differences of nationality, language, and culture, and to initiate its members into a world community. An Episcopalian is made vividly aware of the reality of this fact by the constant recollection of his membership in the Anglican Communion.

What a warming sense of acceptance and fellowship there is in the discovery, for example, thousands of miles from home in Westminster Abbey, St. George's Cathedral in Jerusalem, or a parish church in New Zealand of familiar prayers, canticles, and a pattern of ordered worship and sacramental life which is one's own familiar spiritual nourishment! The contributions of the English-speaking peoples of the world continue to grow in range and importance. The Anglican Communion is the chief religious expression of the life of English-speaking people, and its Book of Common Prayer will be in use as a matter of course wherever the English tongue is spoken. Of course, in some parts of the Anglican Communion the liturgy has been translated into other languages on the original principle that the services should always be "in a language understanded of the people." But in such places, even if one does not understand the native language, and where new liturgical forms and ceremonial practices have been introduced, there is still a real sense of familiarity in the patterns of liturgical and sacramental worship and life.

The history of the development of this great Christian tradition has been traced by some unthinking or unfriendly critics to Henry VIII. Since it seems inevitable that a discussion of this monarch, his marital tastes and practices and his ecclesiastical accomplishments, arises whenever Anglicanism is discussed, perhaps this is a place in this book for a brief exercise in church history! All Anglicans resent the crediting of Henry VIII with the foundation of their communion, not only because it is thoroughly bad history but because it reflects a special definition of the catholic church which Anglicanism has always denied. Ever since William the Conqueror, the Church of England had been in more or less continuous controversy with the Bishop of Rome, to whom Roman Catholics give the title of Pope. This controversy found expression in laws, for example, which denied the right of the Papacy to nominate bishops in England and which forbade appeals from English church courts to any ecclesiastical court outside of the kingdom. Admittedly, this legislation, which was passed in the middle of the 14th century, had become a dead letter, but it indicates the ambition for autonomy and freedom which had animated the English church long before Henry VIII's time. No one I have ever met would want to defend this monarch's marital record, although it must be confessed that in the course which brought about the assertion of the Church of England's independence of Rome, he had a fairly good point in his favor. The truth was that his marriage to Catherine of Aragon had been undertaken in violation of church law with the special permission of the Pope himself. Henry doubted—admittedly somewhat later when he had found what seemed to him a more suitable bride—the legality of the former Pope's action. His doubts, incidentally, were supported by an important group among the leading theological scholars and canon lawyers of his day.

The significant point is that when he declared the Church of England to be essentially autonomous and independent from the jurisdiction of the Pope he did nothing to alter its essential character nor even to disturb the ordinary course of its life. Most of the bishops continued to hold their sees, most of the clergy retained their benefices and parish responsibilities, most of the people worshiped on the Sunday after Parliament had declared Henry VIII to be the supreme head of the Church of England in very much the same way that they worshiped the Sunday before.

Anglicans themselves, obviously, would insist that all that occurred either under Henry, his son Edward VI, or under Elizabeth I, was that the church underwent a period of reformation, thoroughgoing and drawing its inspiration both from the continental Protestant Reformation and from the tradition of Renaissance Humanism. The distinguishing marks of the communion which received such important influences from these events is the burden of many chapters of this book. We proudly claim the tradition of English-speaking Christianity. From St. Patrick through the heroic names of Anselm, Thomas Cranmer, William Laud, John Wesley, John Henry Newman, and a whole host of contemporary Anglican leaders, the Anglican Communion has received a rich and goodly heritage, despite the fact that some of these ancestors have separated themselves finally from her fellowship and communion. Into this proud heritage, every Episcopalian enters by virtue of baptism and confirmation. The marks of these heroes and many other lesser known saints of the past are found in the church's prayer book, hymnal, and body of canon law. Not as a dead curiosity from the past, but as a living and present spiritual resource, the Anglican tradition is inevitably one of the glories of being an Episcopalian.

The spread of Anglican influence, of course, still goes on. With vigor and enthusiasm, the Episcopal Church in America, for example, carried on a widespread missionary activity which still continues, though with far stronger emphasis on local initiative, local authority, and indigenous leadership. With the closing of China as a missionary field after the Communists came to power there, the American Episcopal Church lost one of its traditionally important centers of missionary activity. However, work continued in other areas of strategic importance. One of the most exciting was in the Philippines. A small but impressive missionary activity began there with the American occupation of the islands after the Spanish-American War. This activity, in deference to already established Christian work, was at first limited to American citizens and to hitherto unevangelized mountain tribes. However, in later years the Episcopal Church moved into a position of prominence and is now an autonomous province of the Anglican Communion. The Philippine church has had close and fraternal relationships with the Philippine Independent Church, one of the major non-Roman Catholic bodies in the Islands. The American Episcopal Church bestowed the apostolic succession upon the bishops of the Philippine Independent Church in a history-making service of consecration held in 1950. The Episcopal Seminary in the Philippines has trained a large number of the new clergy of the Philippine Independent Church, and it is confidently expected that closer and closer relationships will develop between the two. Another major area of missionary activity has been Central and South America. From Panama as a center, work spread north and south. Among many dramatic developments the church in Brazil, originally a small diocese, has blossomed into a full fledged province with vigorous activity and growth.

The supervision and support of the missionary enterprise of the Episcopal Church centers in the headquarters building at 815 Second Avenue in New York City.

Since one of the traditional roles of the bishop has been the extension of the church within the boundaries of his jurisdiction, the missionary work of the Episcopal Church centers around her missionary bishops. Some of them have been great and famous Christian heroes, such as Samuel Schereschewsky, the great scholar-bishop of China, and Peter Trimble Rowe, the pioneer bishop of Alaska. It is the responsibility of a missionary bishop, with the support of a budget provided him in part by the national church and in part from his own people, to shepherd the Episcopalians within his district and to seek out opportunities to plant the church in new places and to extend the boundaries and effectiveness of the Episcopal Church's influence. In the Caribbean, in Liberia, in Alaska, in Honolulu, in the Philippines, in many parts of South America, and in many sparsely settled areas of the American Far West, the Episcopal Church has been symbolized by one of the successors of the Apostles, who could claim that succession not only by reason of the laying on of hands but by reason of the brave and adventuresome apostolic task which he daily undertook.

Early in its career the American Episcopal Church made an important decision. In doing so, she turned her back on a venerable tradition of the Church of England which encouraged the foundation of missionary societies. To the Society for the Propagation of the Gospel the American colonies owed the first establishment of the Anglican Communion in this country. Later the Church Missionary Society carried the Christian gospel into many remote and difficult places. The American Episcopal Church decided to stake its future on a bolder idea. That was that the whole church must consider itself a missionary society. The proclamation of the gospel and the extension of its saving and transforming influence in the lives of men and women is not an elective which a few deeply committed members of the church may choose as a special form of spiritual exercise. It is the inevitable responsibility of every baptized person. This identification of the work of mission with the total structure of the church has proved to be an inspired decision. It has kept the missionary activity of the church responsive to the will and purpose of the total membership and has virtually ruled out the possibility of competitive missionary activities representing the various ecclesiastical and theological points of view within the church. In recent years, when missionary groups with different objectives have formed, their unifying commitment to mission has led them to support each other and to work together through the Episcopal Council for Global Mission. As the national church's budget decreased in the 1990's and mission funds became less readily available, the council and like-minded individuals determined to help the church—and its General Convention—find ways to continue the commitment of the church to be a missionary society.

Admittedly, the concept of mission work as the Episcopal Church's primary responsibility was very late in developing due to the preoccupation of the early Episcopalians after the Revolutionary War with the problems of reorganization and the even more formidable task of commending to the new nation a form of Christianity which had been associated with England. That was a serious handicap in the newly independent country that was often impatient of reminders of its former colonial status.

Not until 1833 did the Episcopal Church begin to take its missionary responsibilities with real seriousness. As a result its spread in the United States itself was spotty and erratic. An examination of church statistics reveals that the church is numerically strongest on the Atlantic Seaboard but much weaker in parts of the Middle West that were settled before 1835. In the Rocky Mountains and in the Far West, however, the Episcopal Church is significantly stronger numerically. The Episcopal Church was too late in reaching Kentucky, Indiana, or Missouri, but it arrived with the pioneers in the Rocky Mountain states and on the Pacific slope. It is a nationwide church, and there is no important city in America where there is not a vigorous and thriving parish. A good start, a near collapse after the Revolution, a slow recovery, a surprising burst of activity in the last hundred years—this is a brief sketch of the missionary impulse of American Anglicanism. Many of us feel that it has yet to make its major impact upon American life, and that its days of greater influence lie ahead of it.

It is sustained, however, by its worldwide contacts and sense of Anglican fellowship. After the Anglican Congress in Toronto in 1963 there were vigorous efforts to stimulate this sense through a program with the title "Mutual Responsibility and Interdependence in the Body of Christ." Many pairs of dioceses throughout the world were linked together for a period of time, not to exceed six years, during which by visits back and forth, by mutual programs of education and helpfulness, a very deep sense of common mission and witness and ministry grew and flourished. This, rather than the former rather condescending and patronizing "lady bountiful" spirit of the 19th century missionary enterprise, came to mark the world-wide Anglican family and brought greater dignity and equality of status to peoples and nations and races who once were thought of as "souls benighted," to quote a popular missionary hymn of the earlier era. The change was made dramatic for this writer at the opening service of the 1968 Lambeth Conference when the African delegations of bishops entered Canterbury Cathedral in procession. Almost all of them, except from the Province of South Africa, were black. Many of them were obviously moved deeply by this their first view of the Mother Church of the Anglican Communion. They entered, however, as respected and acknowledged Christian leaders, expected to meet, converse, debate, and vote with their colleagues from the rest of the world as fully equal in status and dignity. It was a picture of a great Christian Communion come of age. Now, by far, the greatest growth of the Anglican Communion is in Africa, and white Anglicans are a minority in the worldwide church.

So the Anglican church has grown beyond the bounds of the British Isles, has passed to America where it has become thoroughly at home, and indeed has been carried to the uttermost parts of the earth. To be an Episcopalian is to have the stimulating sense of living in this ancient and venerable tradition of British Christianity, now become indigenous on every continent and in an astonishing variety of languages and cultures. "From the rising of the sun even unto the going down of the same" Christ is worshiped and his gospel preached and the life of the apostolic church continued in its essentials. Here is one of the deepest satisfactions of being an Episcopalian.

Ten

The Parish

It seems rather late in this book to say something so perfectly obvious, but one of the attractive things about the Episcopal Church is the Episcopalians one gets to know! To begin life in the Episcopal Church as a choirboy may not be a typical introduction to an Episcopal congregation, for he is likely to be unduly flattered and made over, especially by ladies of the congregation with a strong maternal instinct. The fact is that I was figuratively—and sometimes literally—embraced with unmistakable affection when I first made my bow as an Episcopal choirboy. And this may be the reason why I have never seen much justice in the characterization of the typical Episcopal congregation as cold and distant and aloof. It must be admitted, of course, that the Episcopal Church bears the marks of its English background, and that one of these marks is a kind of reserve and formality which can sometimes be mistaken by the demonstrative American as coldness and hauteur. But just as I have never really found the English unfriendly, so I have never believed that Episcopalians were less generously supplied with the milk of human kindness than other religious people. The tradition by which the church is reserved for worship, of course, discourages hearty greetings and neighborly chatting within its walls, although this tradition has been much modified by innovations in liturgy and ceremonial which have created an easier informality. We have already pointed out that one of the important ways in which the Episcopal Church creates the mood of worship among its people is by the custom of spending some time in prayer in preparation for the beginning of the service. The spectacle of people coming quietly into the church, kneeling down, saying their prayers, and then sitting quietly reading through the hymnal or prayer book suggests just as important a truth about the Christian life as does the spectacle of hearty and cheerful greetings and conversation among the assembling congregation.

In most parishes a stranger will find a quiet but genuine welcome from the usher and, as he leaves the church, from the clergyman and others of the congregation. The cheerful custom of a coffee hour after the service—a custom dubbed by a friend of mine "thirst after righteousness"—has made its appearance almost everywhere and aids greatly in creating an atmosphere of friendliness and welcome. It is important, however, not to confuse ordinary congeniality with the supernatural unity and fellowship based upon Christian love which is the distinctive mark of the Christian church. Someone has pointed out that although we are obliged to love our neighbors, nobody can possibly require that we like them! This is, perhaps, to overstate the point, but there is a kind of false heartiness and self-conscious fellowship which sometimes intrudes itself into a Christian congregation but which has as little as possible to do with the real bond of Christian love which unites a congregation made up of diversified temperaments and attitudes. Like all other churches, the Episcopal Church provides any number of opportunities for expressing fellowship, but it must be confessed that oftentimes such organizations are based more on similarity of social status, educational background and temperament than they are upon a deep understanding of what it means to be accepted and to accept others in Christ.

It has been my privilege to serve parishes which drew upon a very wide variety of people to make up their membership. In several cases we have included within one fellowship several millionaires as well as a great many manual laborers, small shopkeepers, school teachers and almost every variety of social background and occupation. At the center of such a variegated fellowship of people is, however, one central and saving relationship, expressed in the sacrament of the Holy Communion. In one parish of mine, for example, two of the people who frequently came to the early celebration of the Holy Communion on

Sunday mornings were one of the leading bankers of the metropolitan area in which the church was located and a laundress from the local hospital. Frequently they knelt side by side at the altar rail, and I was impressed by the unique capacity of the Christian church to establish fellowship over all the natural barriers and divisions of the human family. I don't suppose that, humanly speaking, those two communicants had much in common. Indeed, my guess is that it would have been extraordinarily difficult to have them develop any kind of what the world calls "fellowship" outside of their fellowship at the communion rail. They had very few, if any, interests in common and their backgrounds of education and temperament would make it difficult to communicate whatever similarity of interests might really exist. Their presence together at the altar rail proclaimed, however, that they were equally loved by God and equally used by him for the achievement of his purposes. As C.S. Lewis has pointed out,* the original biblical conception of Christian fellowship is expressed by St. Paul in the simile of the human body. Membership, says Lewis, in a human body is not a matter of being one unit among other similar units, all of them interchangeable one with the other. On the contrary, the members of the human body are unique and irreplaceable and cannot be interchanged. "The eye cannot say unto the hand, I have no need of

*Cf. "Membership" in *The Weight of Glory.*

thee." Obviously, says St. Paul, not all parts of the body are equal in what he calls "honor" nor "comeliness." It ought not to require much observation of the Christian church as it is found in a typical congregation to substantiate St. Paul's conclusions! The wholesale method by which the church reaches out and gathers to herself all who feel the need of her gospel and her life means that of necessity a very mixed bag will result. No other institution in society, of course, attempts to do what the church does in opening her doors wide to allow anyone to come in without any credential whatever. The university with its office of admissions, the country club with its membership committee, the Daughters of the American Revolution with their careful scrutinizing of one's genealogy—all of these are typical of the ways in which the societies of the world create unity and mutuality. The church attempts a more daring experiment. It not only invites everyone in who wants to come; it also proposes to create such a sense of mutuality and communion that the social organism that results must be compared to the family in intimacy and closeness.

At least as well as most other churches I know and a great deal more inclusively than many, the Episcopal Church seems to me to fulfill this ideal of a catholic and universal church. Although I have no statistics to prove this, I have the impression, for example, that a larger percentage of college faculty people belong to the Episcopal Church than to any other single denomination or communion. At the same time, the Episcopal Church has had great success in New York City, as well as in other places, in attracting newly arrived Puerto Ricans into its churches. I also have the impression that the Episcopal Church has more than its quota of eccentrics in its membership! While I may just be reflecting the exasperation of a pastor who has had to deal with the troublesome problem of adjusting such people to the requirements of church life and fellowship, I am inclined to think that this reflects the objectivity of Anglican worship and the wide liberty that is permitted in expressing one's devotion. While I am sure that pastors of other denominations and traditions will rush to defend their reputation for eccentricity also, I am willing to leave it this way, that the Episcopal Church has as wide a variety of people within its membership as any other Christian body on the face of the earth. Perhaps one of the reasons why Episcopalians have gained the unenviable title of "God's frozen people" is that in addition to the English tradition of reserve in personal relationships, there is also oftentimes wider disparity in an Episcopal congregation of economic, educational, and social status than exists in at least many other protestant churches.

Like any other body of American Christians, Episcopalians, of course, express their essential unity with one another in a wide variety of organizations and societies. In an earlier time one of the most impressive organizations in a parish was likely to be the Woman's Auxiliary. Before World War II women usually were barred from positions on the policy-making bodies at both the national and local level; through the Auxiliary they could express their Christian commitment to discipleship and service. This organization's usefulness to the clergy and their services to the parishes where they were established are beyond calculation. The imagination staggers at the number of dinners, the miles of knitting, the assortment of rummage, the gallons of tea and coffee, the electricity employed in pressing and ironing, and all the other statistics that might be compiled about the contribution of the women of the Episcopal Church to its program and life. More important, however, than this discipleship of Martha was the discipleship of Mary which was the Woman's Auxiliary exemplified. It was the single most effective organization for adult education in the Episcopal Church. Bible classes, study courses in missions, lectures on civic and community problems which challenge the Christian conscience—these and any number of other projects designed to help the churchwoman understand more deeply her faith and her church go to make up the educational record of this remarkable organization.

The Episcopal Church Women now carries on much of the work of the Woman's Auxiliary, but today women are serving at almost all levels of the Episcopal Church—vestries, lay readers, diocesan conventions, Standing Committees, diocesan councils, General Convention and all its committees and commissions, and as deacons, priests and bishops.

No mention of women's work would be complete without a reference to its superlative record of missionary giving as expressed through the United Thank Offering. The offering has its origin in the familiar Christian experience of gratitude and thanksgiving. Every woman in a parish (and now more and more men are accepting this discipline) is urged to accept a "Blue Box," a familiar sight in the kitchen of many Episcopal homes. Into this Blue Box go special offerings from time to time when one is moved to thank God for all his many mercies. Twice a year the contents of these boxes are presented at the altar of the parish church in connection with a celebration of the Holy Communion or at one of the other services.

The climax comes in the presentation of the total offering for the past three years at the time of the triennial General Convention. In recent years the offering has risen till it now represents several millions of dollars, and the distribution of this gift to assist in the mission and program of the church is one of the major business responsibilities of the triennial meeting of the women of the church. One of the great breakthroughs in the empowerment program for racial minorities proposed at the 1967 Seattle convention was when the women presented a large sum of money (over two million dollars) to the Presiding Bishop for this purpose in response to his opening sermon. For many years one of the major sources of funds for capital expansion in the mission fields, for example, has come from this gift of the women. One thrills to belong to a church which can claim in such a dramatic way the loyalty and devotion of its women.

A number of other women's organizations exist within the general framework of the Episcopal Church Women, and in many places independent women's organizations have grown up. The Daughters of the King, as an example of the latter, is a well established and widely useful organization, stressing the development of the spiritual life of women and of personal service to the rector and parish. The Church Periodical Club is another organization of established reputation and wide usefulness, having as its objective the distribution of religious periodicals and literature. Time fails to mention the many clubs, guilds, circles and leagues by which the women of the Episcopal Church express their loving loyalty to Christ and their fellowship one with another.

The men of the church never matched the women in the efficiency of their organization nor the dramatic character of their service and contribution to the church's life and program. The increasing role of women in business and in professions would suggest that such exclusively male organizations do not have much of a future. What does stand out as a great opportunity and responsibility is the need for mature Christian reflection by men and women alike on issues of morality and ethics in the total life of church and community.

What is the role of Christian ethics, for example, in the conduct of American business? Obviously, this is not a question which the average parish priest will be able to do very much to illuminate. Priests live, for the most part, above the struggle for business survival and success and with the best will in the world must very largely leave this question to the prayerful thinking of the laity of the church. To ask most Christians to discuss these questions, however, is usually to be met by a blank uncomprehending look or an unconvincing set of platitudes. The truth is that the ethical tradition of the church has a great deal to say about the meaning of Christianity in economic and business life, and it is therefore something of a tragedy that this Christian tradition is so little discussed or reflected on as our nation and world find themselves in new and unexpected crises, of which the emergence of words and phrases like "ecology" and "energy crisis" are symbols. The laity are often encouraged to express their devotion to the church only by the performance of practical but essentially menial tasks. They supervise, in many cases, the buildings and grounds of the parish, its finances, its publicity, and they give their services gladly as ushers, choir members, participants in the every member canvass, and in many other useful and practical ways. The task of adult education is one of the unmet responsibilities of the late 20th century church.

Much less widespread is the existence of special activities for elderly people within the fellowship of the church. Here and there in the Episcopal Church groups of senior citizens are being drawn together, reflecting the obvious fact that in our society the number of elderly people is increasing and that because of developments in medical science they are living on with extraordinary vigor and energy. Any organized program for elderly people needs, however, special wisdom and preparation, and until more attention is given to these matters in pastoral theology in our seminaries the program will not realize its full possibilities.

Perhaps the highest expression of the possibilities of Christian community are realized in what has been traditionally known as the "religious life." Many people, including life-long Episcopalians, frequently ask in open-mouthed astonishment, "Does the Episcopal Church have monks and nuns?" The answer, of course, is that we do. Protestant prejudice against religious orders is probably attributable in large part to the prejudice of Martin Luther. For him monasticism was a denial of the gospel and of the Christian view of the world. He felt strongly about it, because the monasticism he had known seemed to suggest that it was in the multiplication of special acts of devotion and in the performance of the special vows of the monastic that one gained God's favor and earned God's forgiveness. Luther also reacted strongly against the implied disparagement of marriage which he thought monasticism involved. For whatever reasons, he condemned monasticism as a wholly unwarranted Christian vocation, and protestantism generally followed his lead. Even Henry VIII, who was by no means a follower of Lutheran ideas as a rule, suppressed the monastic orders in England and with the proceeds of this expropriation of funds and properties created most of the titled nobility to be found in contemporary England.

Except for a few scattered attempts to revive the monastic life in modified form of which the experiment at Little Gidding in the 17th century was a peculiarly attractive example, Anglicanism knew nothing of monasticism until the Oxford Movement of the 1830's and 1840's. As a part of the new interest in church traditions of the past, the Anglo-Catholics encouraged the re-establishment of Anglican monastic orders. Naturally this movement soon spread to the Episcopal Church in the United States. Father James Huntington, for example, persuaded Bishop Potter of New York to receive his profession of vows as a novice and thus establish the Order of the Holy Cross on November 25, 1884. Although the public outcry was considerable and sharply critical both of Father Huntington and Bishop Potter, the order nevertheless grew and prospered and remains today one of the leading communities for men in the Episcopal Church. My own experience both with the Order of the Holy Cross and with the Sisters of the Holy Nativity and the Sisters of the Transfiguration—to name the religious orders of which I have had personal experience—leads me to the conviction that they are mainly free from the assumptions that offended Luther and that a reformed monasticism is as conceivable as the reformation of any other aspect of the Christian tradition. At its best, monasticism may represent a desire of men and women to take upon themselves, as Bishop Potter expressed it in defense of his actions in receiving Father Huntington's vows, "the soldier life and the soldier rule, turning their backs on home and gain in a self-directed life . . . Is poverty inconsistent with the Christian calling? Is the unmarried state? Is obedience to a daily rule of prayer and work?" Bishop Potter went on to voice the hope that the Order of the Holy Cross, and by inference other monastic orders both for men and women that might be established, "might do a John the Baptist work." The life of the religious communities remains one of the least known aspects of the life of the Episcopal Church, and yet it has a potential attraction for many men and women who would respond to the challenge and discipline that it involves. Certainly for the church to have before its eyes the spectacle of a company of men and women who have renounced worldly positions, the normal satisfactions of marriage and family life and the privilege of self-direction and absolute liberty of choice, not because they think these things inherently wicked in themselves but that they are willing to renounce them in order to be free to serve God in special circumstances and special ways, is surely a healthy thing in an age when the church is too easily beguiled by the ways of the world and too readily adapts its rigorous ethic to whatever is comfortable and fashionable.

So I am an Episcopalian in large part because I have known other Episcopalians. They have invited me, welcomed me, instructed me, inspired me, and as a fellowship of people, more united by their common acceptance of Christ's forgiveness and their common acceptance of responsibility as his disciples than by natural affinity or congeniality, they have shown me something of what St. Paul meant by "the Body of Christ." I do not say, of course, that they have not often irritated me, dismayed me, appalled me, and even sometimes bored me! But since I must have often created the same impression on them, perhaps it is just another way of demonstrating the profundity and strength of our fellowship one with another.

Eleven

Education

Like most other Christian bodies down through twenty centuries, the Episcopal Church teaches and practices infant baptism; and like most other Christian bodies the Episcopal Church has had to wrestle with some of the difficulties which this policy raises. Infant baptism can be justified primarily on sociological and psychological grounds. Observably, human beings can and repeatedly do receive all kinds of privileges and benefits from groups into which they are initiated long before they can make any independent decision about such membership or indeed are even consciously aware of it. All kinds of unnoticed—and therefore even more powerful—influences mould attitudes, determine values, condition behavior, as a result of even a very small child's participation in the life of a family or of a neighborhood or of a nation. The Christian church has overwhelmingly accepted the lesson of this human experience, and infants have been baptized since the time when whole families began to be converted and brought into the church.

Christian life, as the New Testament describes it, is not, however, only a matter of a passive reception of unconscious and unnoticed influences, benefits, and privileges. One is not a member of the church in just the same way he is a member of other social groups. One of the characteristic requirements of Jesus of Nazareth in his teaching was that a person make a decisive commitment of trust and faith and self-conscious obedience as a prerequisite of following him. This kind of decisive commitment not only may, but often does, demand a radical disassociation from the past and from even its most precious and intimate influences. "Except a man leave his father and mother he cannot be my disciple." How does the practice and doctrine of infant baptism make room for this emphasis of the gospel upon radical decision and commitment? In traditional theology the full benefits of a sacrament can only be realized as the recipient opens heart, mind, life to all that the Holy Spirit offers and makes available in that sacrament. What does this mean with respect to infant baptism?

A classical answer in western Christendom (which means all churches whose practice and doctrine have been strongly influenced by Roman Christianity) was the rite of confirmation. It was by the preparation I was given for receiving confirmation at thirteen years of age that I first was moved to give thoughtful attention to the Episcopal Church. Confirmation has always had an ambiguous position in the Episcopal Church. For reasons which I have never had adequately explained, confirmation was declared to be a hurdle to the reception of the Holy Communion. Presumably this was arranged in order that no one should come to the Holy Communion without a knowledge of what it meant and what participation in it implied. I never saw why this could not be done, however, without all the excitement of the bishop coming and laying hands on my head, but since that guaranteed me a moment of conspicuous attention (plus the gift of a prayer book from my family) who was I to question this unexplained requirement?

I was aware, of course, that confirmation was the way I was to say "yes" to what my parents and godparents had done for me and to me in infant baptism. In the past, the Episcopal Church—and all western catholicism including the Lutheran churches—apparently intended confirmation to be the completion of baptism. This view has been changed in the Episcopal Church with the adoption of the 1979 prayer book: "Holy Baptism is full initiation . . ." I do not object to that for reasons I have indicated above in discussing infant baptism. Surely, however, to be fully and adequately a member of Christ's Body the church demands more than just baptism, at least if that baptism took place in infancy. It must demand, as Christ in the gospel says, a radical and a personal and a decisive commitment to him and a fuller and fuller sharing of his life and spirit. At a time (I would gladly make that plural—at what may perhaps be several critical times) in a person's life there ought to be a public acknowledgment of one's commitment to him in obedience and trust and an acceptance of this pledge by one who represents a wider aspect of the Christian fellowship than just a local congregation—the bishop—who will then pray on behalf of the wider church for a new outpouring of the Holy Spirit in order that these promises now made by a mature adult may be kept and fulfilled. The laying on of hands—an ancient biblical symbol— represents and conveys this power and gift.

The practice of infant baptism and of confirmation sets the stage in the Episcopal Church for an emphasis on Christian nurture and education. Very early in my experience at the Episcopal Church I saw that they took seriously the question of Christian education. Before I could become an Episcopalian I was required to undergo careful instruction about the Episcopal Church's teaching and life. My present recollections of that instruction are very hazy, but the fact that I can remember the rector's remarks about evolution and the doctrine of creation as stated in the creed is, I think, evidence of his ability to communicate to a 13-year-old boy. Perhaps even more lasting and impressive was the training I received in connection with membership in the boys' choir and later on as an acolyte. To take part, Sunday after Sunday, in the worship of the church meant, of course, gaining some knowledge of the meaning of the seasons of the church year, the usage of the prayer book, the significance of certain ceremonial postures and gestures, and a great many other things which initiated me rapidly into the Episcopal Church and gave me the comfortable and smug feeling of being an insider on something quite impressive and important.

In its emphasis upon confirmation, the church obviously is expressing her high estimation of the importance of instruction and education in the meaning of the Christian faith. The traditional form of confirmation instruction—a course of a few weeks—is obviously not a very realistic way to respond to this need. When I recall what I often in my ministry tried to cram into such a brief course I realize how futile the effort was. A rough outline of what I tried to do would run something like this: the church's theological teachings, her attitude toward the Bible, the creeds, tradition, reason; church history, a sketch of the development of Christianity since our Lord's Resurrection and Ascension, the origin and development of the Church of England, the early days of the Episcopal Church in America, the crisis of the Revolution, and its subsequent growth; the church's ethical teachings, the Christian meaning of marriage and her attitude toward divorce, her discipline of fasting and penitence, the obligations of the laity with respect to church attendance and church support, the church's teaching about society and its relationship to the world; the church's government, its organization, the doctrine of the ministry, highlights of the church's canon law; the missionary program of the church, the rights and responsibilities of the laity in church government; the church's worship, the principles of liturgical worship, the structure and meaning of the choir offices and the occasional offices, ceremonial customs, the church year, the meaning of vestments and church ornaments; the Holy Communion, its meaning and place in the Christian life, doctrines of the presence of Christ in the Holy Communion, preparation for the Holy Communion, ceremonial practices and customs having to do with its observance.

In addition to this rather full outline, I made it a practice to introduce members of the confirmation class to the life of the particular parish into which they were coming by confirmation. Representatives of parish organizations came to explain and describe the various functionings of parochial life. In addition to children who are presented for confirmation in fulfillment of their baptismal vows, there were always, of course, many adults, most of them with some previous religious connections who for one reason or another were seeking to know more about the Episcopal Church and on the basis of what they discovered seeking to be confirmed members of it. In every parish in which I have ever served, the confirmation classes presented to the bishop contained almost always as many or more adults than children. In one case an advertisement inserted for only one

Sunday in a metropolitan newspaper with the heading "Why Not Be An Episcopalian?" brought nearly 150 people to the first meeting of the class. The title of the ad sounds a little brash as I look back on it, and as a bishop who saw it exclaimed, "Well, why not?" But the results obviously show that a great many people in that metropolitan area were seeking some religious affiliation and were ready to respond to an invitation to find out something about one of the main traditions of Christendom.

In theory, the provision for confirmation instruction is a way of demonstrating the church's concern that her membership shall be an informed one. In practice, however, a "once in a lifetime" cram course just before confirmation will not do much to bring about that result. The Christian view of history implies that learning about things having to do with God and his church can have no end, for new situations are always arising in which the meaning and relevance of the Christian faith must be freshly discovered and applied. Much has been said about the religious illiteracy of our time, and the Episcopal Church has had its full share. The experience of military chaplains in the Second World War indicated the shocking ignorance on the part of people of all churches, or of none, about the most elementary matters having to do with the Bible and the Christian faith. Against such widespread ignorance and even lack of interest, a few sessions of a confirmation class are, of course, woefully inadequate as preparation for a thorough understanding and grounding in Christian knowledge.

What about the Sunday school? I had very little experience as a pupil in the Episcopal Sunday school, but I spent several exciting years during my time in college as a teacher. In this experience I was introduced to some of the possibilities but also some of the frustrations of a Sunday school. The parish where I belonged at the time had several leaders in the public schools in the community among its members, and the rector enlisted one of them to train us as teachers. It was an exciting and demanding experience. We were introduced to some of the current educational theories and especially to the undeniable fact that a person learns best that in which he is genuinely interested, which means when his own needs and problems are involved. In this Sunday school great stress was laid upon the totality of learning which took place within the whole experience of the teacher and child. Habits of reverence and worship in church, habits of thoughtfulness and consideration in class—these counted for just as much as the amount of information acquired. On the other hand, this was no faddism, which suggested that the intellectual content of the Christian tradition was of no importance. The natural interest and skills of children were, however, enlisted for the learning process. Although this was before the advent of audio-visual aids, creative use of art, music, and dramatics marked the curriculum, and many promising innovations were developed.

The problem of the Sunday school remains, however, an extraordinarily difficult one. The problem of providing, for example, for suitable space, properly equipped, for the purpose of teaching children for only one or two hours a week is a staggering economic problem just in itself. Trained and competent teachers are, of course, few and far between and notoriously difficult to pin down to a regular Sunday after Sunday responsibility, let alone to the preparation time demanded. It has been estimated that children enrolled in Sunday school are usually absent about forty percent of the time. What would the public schools be able to do with an attendance record as poor as that? The Episcopal Church tried to face some of these problems in the development of a new curriculum in the 1950's and has made some promising suggestions, looking toward a solution. Parents, for example, ought to be deeply involved in the whole teaching and learning process. On the whole, however, one must confess that the developments in the Episcopal Church's programs in Christian education, not only in the Sunday school, have not yet come to grips with the depth and seriousness of the problem. Promising experiments are few and far between. The educational emphasis of the 1950's which sought to relate biblical and theological content to recognized human situations and felt needs and perplexities was a right one, but the adequacy of clergy and lay leaders to do this is a serious question.

Perhaps the most hopeful educational effort in recent years in the Episcopal Church has been the involvement of both adults and children in a combination of worship and learning as a normal Sunday morning experience. In this connection, an action of the Houston General Convention of 1970 has considerable significance. The decision that was made there was to admit children to the Holy Communion at the earliest possible age, certainly before confirmation. If what we have said of infant baptism at the outset of this chapter is true, then logically the members of the Christian family ought regularly to have the incorporating experience of eating with the family at its common meal. Preparation for children and their parents to do this easily and knowledgeably is now part of the pastoral ministry in many Episcopal churches, and its value as a way to recognize and come to grasp the meaning of the church's great sacrament of the Holy Communion has already been extensively demonstrated. After (or perhaps better, before) this sacramental celebration both adults and children are involved in more explicit sessions of Christian education. The church at study as well as the church at worship is an important emphasis in the biblical tradition which often extols "wisdom"—indeed more often than it extols "piety!"

Developments up to the present indicate, however, several important things about the Episcopal Church's attitude toward the task of educating her children. In the first place, she regards education as a far more profound development than the acquisition of information. In the second place, she believes that the Christian faith can best be understood in terms of the real life situations in which boys and girls and men and women find themselves. In the third place, she recognizes the role of the family and the Christian home as a teaching agency. Fourthly, she has set an admittedly high standard for teachers and demanded a generous investment of time and money on the part of the parish and of its leadership for the educational task.

One of the important means for Christian education is the extensive program which the Episcopal Church carries on in elementary and secondary education, traditionally in boarding schools but increasingly through the use of a parochial system. It would be unfortunate, of course, if this development involved any loss of interest in maintaining the quality of publicly supported education in the communities of America. The troublesome problems that arise, however, in dealing with religion in the public schools under the usual interpretation that has prevailed of the meaning of the principle of the separation of church and state have limited the effectiveness of the public schools in the eyes of many church people. There is much to provoke thought in the observation of the late Archbishop Temple of Canterbury that one cannot omit from the education which goes on five days in the week all mention of God and then suddenly introduce him for one hour on Sunday without suggesting that he is essentially irrelevant to the whole business of life! Many thorny problems bristle in this area, but at least the Episcopal Church's deep concern for the religious training of her children is evident in the vigorous provision she is making through the parochial school program.

The parochial schools, of course, are simply carrying further an interest in secondary education that has always been characteristic of the Episcopal Church, especially in its long-established centers. Under more or less direct church auspices hundreds of secondary and preparatory schools are carrying on programs throughout the United States. Some of them like Groton, St. Paul's, Kent, and Choate have famous and enviable reputations. Their contribution to the vigor and life of the Episcopal Church cannot be questioned. Although the religious interests of another generation differ very considerably from our own, one cannot deny the influence for good exerted by an Endicott Peabody of Groton or a Samuel S. Drury of St. Paul's. A recent biographer of Franklin Delano Roosevelt, a Groton graduate who was conspicuously devoted to Endicott Peabody, writes, for example, about Roosevelt: "He believed in doing good, in showing other people how to do good, and he assumed that ultimately people would do good. By 'good' he meant the Ten Commandments and the Golden Rule, as interpreted by Endicott Peabody."*

*Burns, James MacGregor, *Roosevelt, The Lion and the Fox* (Harcourt, Brace. 1956), page 475.

If Groton taught Franklin Roosevelt a deep loyalty to his church, it obviously taught him something important. But, of course, the theological revolution of the third and fourth decades of this century has left its mark also upon the Episcopal Church's secondary schools, and there is increasing evidence of a willingness to wrestle with deep questions of theology and their relevance to the responsibilities of secondary education.

The reader will not be surprised in view of my past experience as the chaplain of a famous university to hear that I believe that one of the great opportunities before the Episcopal Church and one in which it is realizing ever more fully its possibilities is the whole field of work on the campuses of our colleges and universities. Surprisingly enough, in view of the prominence which the universities of Cambridge and Oxford played in the history of the Church of England, very few Anglican institutions of higher learning in America survive to the present day. There are still ten colleges and universities, at home and abroad, which continue today as accredited institutions of higher learning directly under the sponsorship and control of the Episcopal Church. Several colonial colleges, notably Columbia University and the College of William and Mary, had Anglican influences in their beginnings and early history, but no direct control by the Episcopal Church is provided at the present time.

The church's record of work in universities and

colleges blossomed in vigorous development after the First World War. Much of the enthusiasm for this work was due to the pioneering labors of the Church Society for College Work and the willingness of a few clergy and laity of broad vision to make the college ministry a matter of high priority. Part of the reason, of course, was that the percentage of Episcopal students in colleges far exceeded—in some cases more than double—the percentage of Episcopalians in the population as a whole. As some wag observed, "Episcopalians are denser in colleges than elsewhere."

In its earlier days, it is perhaps not unfair to say the main preoccupation of the college chaplain to Episcopal students was to retain their loyalty to the church or to convert outsiders to the church against the unfavorable tide of thinking and opinion which characterized the campus as a whole. Due in large part, however, to the growing concern of the college chaplain with Episcopal faculty personnel, this tendency has shown a gradual diversification of direction. It is now recognized that Anglican theology gives the character of divine vocation to the scholarly pursuit of the campus and that the Episcopal Church's ministry, therefore, is not only to rescue people from the temptations of their academic calling and environment but to transform their whole outlook upon their academic work. The Christian faith, after all, is in the God of creation, the God who moves and works in nature and in history. Every genuine discovery of truth must, therefore, be seen as a new revelation of the character and mind of God. All learning is potentially theological in its meaning. One of the main responsibilities of the Episcopal Church's ministry to the campus is to make this truth clear.

The revival of religious studies in the contemporary American college and university is an unmistakable sign of the times. Departments and courses in religion have sprung up on all sides. This burgeoning growth represents an enormous opportunity for the church. Especially to an Episcopalian, with his background of a tradition of religious humanism and of the validity of human reason as one of the ways in which he can know God, the scholarly study of religion, marked by the same sharpness of inquiry and rigor of method which is found in any other of the academic disciplines, can help create a well informed and theologically articulate laity.

A generation ago the hope was held forth that by the Episcopal Church's ministry to the campus it could save a few college students for the church. Now the possiblity is dawning that the ministry of the Episcopal Church on the college and university campus may, as a matter of fact, save the church itself by raising it to new levels of relevance and self-awareness. It would not, of course, be the first time in church history that the church's life had been revitalized from the college campus or its equivalent. The Lutheran Reformation began at a university, so did the Evangelical Revival, so did the Tractarian

Movement of the 1830's. Is it too much to hope that the predominance of theological interest on the contemporary college campus, the attention given to religious issues and the great world traditions of religious experience, will bring new theological sharpness and clarity to our churches through the young men and women who graduate from our universities and colleges in these next few years? Fortunately, the vigor and vitality of the Episcopal Church's ministry to the college campus puts it in a strategic position to make maximum use of this new development.

Only slowly did the Episcopal Church realize the possibilities of teaching her faith and demonstrating the quality of her life by means of some of the new techniques of mass communication. The Episcopal Church's tradition of a full use of the arts and drama and architecture, of music and pageantry, suggest that it could make unusually effective use of the television media. The Christmas service telecast from the Washington Cathedral for many years is a notable example. The same opportunity would appear to exist in the realm of religious books. The work of such English Anglicans as C.S. Lewis and Dorothy Sayers has reached a wide audience. Among American Episcopalians none has achieved quite the eminence of their English counterparts, but some American writers give promise of seizing for the Episcopal Church the opportunity represented in the present interest in religion and the corresponding high tide of sales of religious books.

The enormous educational task that rests upon the modern priest points, of course, to the importance of a well trained ministry and to the strategic role which the seminaries and divinity schools of the church will play in shaping its future. After the Second World War the number of candidates for the ministry multiplied impressively. Many churches (including the Episcopal Church) had more persons offering themselves for the ministry than could be employed. In recent years enrollment in Episcopal seminaries has tended to decline.

Unlike most other religious bodies, the Episcopal Church only relatively recently sought to have official responsibility for the support or the standards of its theological training schools. Only the General Theological Seminary in New York City has any relationship whatever to the General Convention, and this relationship is a very limited one whereby the convention elects certain members of the Board of Trustees and the seminary makes a report every three years to the convention. Some other seminaries have a similar connection with a diocese or with a group of dioceses or in some cases with the provincial synod. A Board for Theological Education extends or withholds a quasi-official recognition of a theological seminary according to whether it meets the minimum standards of the American Association of Theological Schools. A seminary, however, which does not meet the standards is nevertheless perfectly free to continue to exist as long as it can recruit a faculty and student body. Given the different traditions and schools of thought which are represented within the Episcopal Church, this *laissez faire* attitude toward theological education is perhaps inevitable and may provide a salutary kind of competition and specialization. Indications are, however, that as enrollment numbers, parish vacancies, and seminary operating costs become problems, that far more centralized planning will be required. Many Episcopalians feel that the church ought to take official cognizance of the seminaries in a more thoroughgoing way than is now the case, setting standards and guaranteeing adequate support.

The ultimate responsibility for determining the adequacy of the preparation of a candidate for the ministry is left up to the bishop of his diocese and the Commission on the Ministry (including in some dioceses the traditional board of examining chaplains). The candidate for ordination often complains about this system and about the difficulty of following up his preparation for the successful completion of his seminary course with another preparation—which may be very different in character—for passing the General Ordination Examination. As all students know, the passing of examinations is an art, consisting partly in a sensitivity to the prejudices and peculiarities of the examiners! Perhaps it is asking a great deal of a candidate for Holy Orders to expect him or her to learn the peculiarities of the seminary faculty and then in addition to guess at the peculiarities of the GOE examiners, the bishop and the diocesan authorities, but this is a fact of life.

By and large the seminaries give thorough consideration to the great areas of theological study: the Old and New Testaments, church history, systematic theology, pastoral theology, liturgics, canon law, Christian ethics and moral theology, and Christian education. If any criticism can be made of the seminaries and divinity schools of the church, perhaps this one is the most justifiable, that they carry on their instruction too much in isolation from the main intellectual and social currents of the world around them. Some of the seminaries by reason of geographical location are cut off from contact with an urban center or a great university. Too little effort is made in the seminary to relate the interests that a student has developed in undergraduate studies to the student's theological training. This of course is no doubt due in part to the wide diversity of undergraduate preparation which a typical seminary student body represents. Some seminaries include courses in "apologetics" or in "the philosophy of religion." Insofar as such courses examine the cultural and intellectual tendencies of our modern world and show the points of similarity and contrast between these tendencies and the presuppositions of the Christian's world outlook, they are fulfilling the kind of requirement that I have in mind. Fortunately, dramatic changes have taken place which promise to enrich and make more exciting the program both of the seminary and of the secular university, to have the two confronting each other from time to time on a scholarly level, debating, differing, agreeing but even under the most unfavorable circumstance facilitating to some extent communication between theology and other intellectual interests of our time.

Most of the seminaries of the Episcopal Church, of course, have concentrated upon training for the parochial ministry. Some provide opportunities for doing advanced scholarly work in the theological studies for persons who have no intention of seeking ordination. The task of training lay persons to think in theological perspective and categories is an exciting new responsibility being put upon seminaries. Another is the responsibility for continuing education for the clergy. It is inconceivable that after five or ten years out of seminary an ordained minister would not need fresh insights, new learnings, and renewed inspiration. Many seminaries of the Episcopal Church have mounted impressive programs designed to meet these needs. The percentage of ordained clergy who take advantage of these—or indeed any similar—programs remains far too low, however, and bishops and vestries need to be made to realize what promise of renewal this program holds for the church.

The Episcopal Church obviously gives high significance to education—for her children, her young people, her adults and her clergy and other full-time professional workers. As we have seen in another chapter, this educational enterprise is allowed to go on without the restrictions of an excessive dogmatism or a biblical literalism but rather on the assumption that the consecrated use of one's intellectual abilities is a justifiable way in which to serve and glorify God. This respect for education is one of the truly impressive characteristics of the Episcopal Church and one in which I have always rejoiced.

Twelve

The Penitent Church

I hope I have not portrayed the Episcopal Church in too generous and rosy a light. As I look back over the preceding chapters the predominant note has been gratitude for the many ways in which this church to which I came as a stranger so many years ago has fulfilled for me the ideals of a Christian community and the Body of Christ. It would not be true, of course, to say that the Episcopal Church always makes me proud of my decision to come into its membership and to enter its ministry. It is easy to think of faults— some of them very serious—about which anyone considering the Episcopal Church as a spiritual home ought to be warned lest he find himself disillusioned. One ought to be realistic, for example, about our record of stewardship. I am not proud of our record of giving for mission programs beyond our boundaries or our per capita giving to the whole program of the national church. Something is terribly wrong with the sense of values of a church that lets the great world opportunities of the 20th century go by without seizing them in the name of Christ, and all because we spend such a large percentage of our gifts and offerings on our own churches and within our own national boundaries. It is embarrassing to report that Episcopalians are among the worst religious and ecclesiastical isolationists in Christendom.

I am not proud either of the attitude of many Episcopalians about cooperative Christianity. As president of a metropolitan Church Federation, I found myself almost alone among the local Episcopal clergy in my support of its program. (Only about five or six Episcopal churches out of a total of 38 in the area served gave even token financial support to our work.) A kind of ecclesiastical snobbishness seems to pervade the Episcopal Church—not blatant and overt as a rule—but operating quietly to frustrate any real commitment to cooperative undertakings. There is a bland assumption that, as a testy old 18th century gentleman is reported to have said, "There may be other ways to be a Christian than in the Episcopal Church, but no gentleman would take advantage of them"! As a church we have done as much as any other body—and much more than most—for the sake of the Ecumenical Movement, but for the most part it remains on the level of top-echelon theological discussion and has little support in the local communities. The difficulties of such local cooperation have already been described. The Episcopal Church represents an appreciation of tradition in an American ecclesiastical world where all history between the New Testament and the landing of the Pilgrims is too often considered fairly irrelevant. It stands for an authoritative ministry among churches that are highly independent and congregational in their conception of government and authority. It has an understanding of catholic life and faith that enables it to appreciate the great Roman Catholic Church in a way that at least until recently has baffled and irritated many protestants. We are a minority among the protestant family of church traditions—although we can often find support from individual leaders and usually from Lutherans and "high-church" Presbyterians. Without compromising for a moment our own position, we might, however, get into the movement for cooperative protestantism with both feet and help to form and direct its development rather than deride it for its one-sidedness and its many mistakes. The smug assumption of all too many Episcopalians that the rest of the protestant world will come to us eventually and that consequently we have no need to go out to meet them is pompous presumption—not to say blasphemy against the Holy Spirit. It is not one of the reasons I am an Episcopalian.

I am distressed also by a subtle pressure for conformity that sometimes hangs like a pall over the Episcopal Church. The Anglican delight in the *via media* (middle way) ought not to be defined as being frozen on dead center. My friends know I love argument and debate, and perhaps I am only justifying and rationalizing my own taste for controversy when I say that I believe in a much more vigorous and sustained interchange between the several schools of thought in the Episcopal Church than often seems to be going on. The *via media*, for me, is an indefinable line that shifts back and forth in the continuing encounter of the Anglo-Catholic, the Evangelical, and the Broad Church parties. I hope I am not pleading for controversy just for controversy's sake, but I do believe that the Episcopal Church is in danger of confusing the unity and godly love which ought always to characterize the church, with the kind of conformity and amiability which is the mark of what we have learned to call the "other-directed" society. It was not always thus. Some of the great controversialists of the past would be most uncomfortable today. It is no compliment to the intensity of our devotion as Episcopalians to be told that we cannot risk controversy and an honest opposition of convictions for fear of rending the church asunder. We like to think of Anglicanism, sometimes, as a "bridge church," linking both catholic and reformed elements in the Christian tradition. I am not sure my metaphor will serve me here, but I would urge that the bridge needs to be firmly anchored on both sides of the supposed chasm! That is to say, I hope we may have a deeply convinced and well-informed and highly articulate catholic party as well as a deeply convinced, well-informed and highly articulate evangelical party, so that we may be kept in the middle way because the demands of truth and comprehensiveness keep us there. If we try to define some "Anglican line" we shall be false to history and our unique calling as a church that has much to teach the Ecumenical Movement about the meaning of a catholic and reformed church which can live in unity without demanding uniformity.

I am glad that we are called upon so regularly by the services of the prayer book to confess our sins—and not just our personal sins but our sins as a church. When we said as we were taught to say in the 1928 prayer book that we have "erred and strayed from thy ways like lost sheep," did we not mean that we have as a church often missed God's calling to us, have ignored the summons he issues to imagination and service, have betrayed the comprehensive and self-forgetful love which called us into existence as his family? Only a church which is humbly aware of its shortcomings can possibly serve to mediate the love of God to the world and so justify its characterization as "the Body of Christ." The penitent church is the best witness to the truth that it is the Holy Living God whom we serve. The fact of our humility proves that we have some genuine knowledge of God himself and have not bowed ourselves before an idol of our own contriving.

So a catalog of failings which can be compiled for the Episcopal Church does not dismay me—although I feel the shame and the rebuke of missed opportunities and wasted potentialities. In my disappointment and resentment, I can remember that the Episcopal Church itself has taught me the real meaning of what a church ought to be, and that I am using the standard of the Prayer Book and the creeds and the Holy Scripture—all of which I know through the Episcopal Church—to call the Episcopal Church into judgment!

This book has been revised twice since its original publication. Much has had to be brought up to date and there have been many changes in these years. Despite my dismay at the Episcopal Church and the ways it often wavers and stumbles, this responsibility of rewriting this book has enormously encouraged me. The Episcopal Church has taken some giant steps forward in my own lifetime and ministry. Not all change, of course, can be equated with progress, and I have seen some foolish and ill-conceived changes appear and soon disappear. But that there is a willingness and a capacity to respond and to grow is always a sign of life. The main elements in the Anglican tradition still have their validity and will continue to have their appeal, but the Episcopal Church is ready to be renewed and reformed, and for all my impatience with the pace of that development, I find events promising for the future. The retiring Archbishop Ramsey of Canterbury wrote these words many years ago about the Anglican Church, and they speak for me and, I believe, many others who find our Christian home in the Episcopal Church: "While the Anglican Church is vindicated by its place in history, with a strikingly balanced witness to Gospel and church and sound learning, its greater vindication lies in its pointing through its own history to something of which it is a fragment. Its credentials are its incompleteness, with the tension and travail in its soul. It is clumsy and untidy, it baffles neatness and logic. For it is sent not to commend itself as 'the best type of Christianity,' but by its very brokenness to point to the universal church wherein all have died."*

By the grace of God, I am also moved oftentimes to reflect that I have failed the Episcopal Church more times than she has failed me, that she corrects my prejudices and one-sidedness, that she steadies my devotion which waxes and wanes with disturbing frequency, that she both rebukes and forgives my sloth and self-indulgence, that she holds before me always a goal of perfection—"that the rest of our life may be pure and holy"—which eludes me perennially but which calls to something deep within me which I am confident cannot forever be denied, that she points me forward to those good things that "pass man's understanding . . . which God has prepared for those who unfeignedly love him." One criticizes a church that has meant so much to him only that it may speak more persuasively and winningly to others and play more effectively its all-important role in the economy of God for his Holy, Catholic, and Apostolic Church which is being realized more fully in

*A.M. Ramsey, *The Gospel and the Catholic Church* (Longmans, 1936), page 220.

the Ecumenical Movement of our time. Without disparaging the witness and work of other branches of the church, I can only bear testimony to my own discovery that in the Episcopal Church I found the most balanced, comprehensive, satisfying, and stimulating experience of Christian faith and Christian life that I can imagine. I became an Episcopalian by a set of fortuitous circumstances, but I am an Episcopalian because in my experience I found there what it means to be a Christian.